MATERIALS FOR THE STUDY OF THE EARLY HISTORY OF THE VAISHNAVA SECT

Owing to the antiquity and rarity of this book, certain pages are regrettably absent, and readability is compromised due to the blurring of the original text. If you possess any insights regarding the availability of these missing sections, kindly inform us. Your assistance is crucial in ensuring the completion of this significant work for the benefit of future generations.

MATERIALS FOR THE STUDY OF THE EARLY HISTORY OF THE VAISHNAVA SECT

BY

HEMCHANDRA RAYCHAUDHURI

GYAN

Published by

Gyan Publishing House
5, Ansari Road
Daryaganj, New Delhi-110002
Phone: 011-47034999, 9811692060
E-mail: books@gyanbooks.com

Distribution Network
gyanbooks.com
India, USA, Canada, UK, Australia

ISBN: 978-93-6280-505-8 (HB)
First Published, 1936

2nd Impression 2024

Printed at: Gyan Press, Delhi.

MATERIALS FOR THE STUDY OF THE EARLY HISTORY OF THE VAISHNAVA SECT

Author: HEMCHANDRA RAYCHAUDHURI

MATERIALS

FOR THE STUDY

OF

THE EARLY HISTORY OF THE VAISHNAVA SECT

MATERIALS FOR THE STUDY OF THE EARLY HISTORY OF THE VAISHNAVA SECT

BY

HEMCHANDRA RAYCHAUDHURI, M.A., PH.D.
CARMICHAEL PROFESSOR AND HEAD OF THE DEPARTMENT OF ANCIENT INDIAN HISTORY AND CULTURE, CALCUTTA UNIVERSITY; AUTHOR OF "POLITICAL HISTORY OF ANCIENT INDIA," "STUDIES IN INDIAN ANTIQUITIES," Etc., JOINT-AUTHOR OF THE "GROUNDWORK OF INDIAN HISTORY."

SECOND EDITION, REVISED AND ENLARGED

PUBLISHED BY THE
UNIVERSITY OF CALCUTTA
1936

To

THE HON'BLE SIR ASUTOSH MOOKERJEE,

KT., C.S.I., M.A., D.L., D.Sc., Ph.D.,

who has raised the Calcutta University

to an eminence

which recalls the palmiest days of

Takshasila and Nalanda,

these Lectures

are humbly dedicated by the Author,

in token of profound admiration and reverence.

EXTRACTS FROM THE PREFACE TO THE FIRST EDITION

The following pages contain a general summary of a course of lectures on the Early History of the Bhāgavata-Vaishṇava sect which I, in the capacity of a Post-Graduate teacher of Ancient Indian History and Culture, delivered to my students during the session 1918-19.

The plan and purpose of the lectures are stated at length in the Foreword, and they need no further comment in the Preface. But it may not be out of place to draw the attention of the reader to just one or two points which ought to be borne in mind in reading through the book.

First, it has not been my intention to write an exhaustive treatise on Early Vaishṇavism. I have been chiefly concerned to indicate the lines on which the future studies in the subject ought to proceed in order to form a clear idea of the development of the different aspects of the Vaishṇava religion and philosophy around the historical nucleus as supplied by the life and teaching of Vāsudeva Kṛishṇa whose personality in its varied conception has been at the back of the religious aspirations of multitudinous sections of the Hindu community. In other words, I have endeavoured to show that the huge fabric of the Vaishṇava religion of love and devotion was not based upon a mythical fancy of the poets, but has a truth in the personal history of Vāsudeva Kṛishṇa which has been overshadowed by the stupendous growth of legends.

* * * *

Secondly, I have to confess that I have not been able to utilise fully the evidence of all the ancient Jaina and Buddhist records.

* * * *

Lastly, I have to say a word about the system of transliteration adopted in the following pages. The system followed is substantially the same as used in the Indian Antiquary. In quotations, however, the original spelling of proper names has usually been retained.

I do not find words adequately to express my gratitude to the Hon'ble Sir Asutosh Mookerjee, President of the Council of Post-Graduate Teaching in Arts, who has never failed in the midst of his many onerous duties to take interest in the progress of the work.

Among my colleagues Dr. Barua and Mr. Chanda have placed me under deep obligation, the former by revising the proofs and offering some valuable suggestions, the latter by permitting me to make use of the Mathurā Bhāgavata Inscription of the time of Śoḍāsa. The credit of discovering the name of Vāsudeva in the China inscription of Yajña Śrī belongs to my pupil Mr. N. G. Majumdar. The indexes have been prepared by Messrs. H. C. Roy and P. C. Bagchi, my pupils.

January 2, 1920. H. C. RAYCHAUDHURI.

PREFACE TO THE SECOND EDITION

The task of revising a work that deals with any aspect of Ancient Indian history and civilisation for a new edition is by no means an easy one. And the difficulties of the reviser are not lessened by the fact that a period of sixteen years intervenes between the first appearance of the volume in print and its reissue in 1936—a period during which numerous treatises, notes and monographs on the subject have appeared in various publications. The writer of these pages is conscious of his own limitations, of the fact that he has, in all probability, not been able to make full use of all these learned disquisitions. But he has endeavoured to the best of his ability to incorporate some of the more important results of recent research, especially in the domain of South Indian history and chronology, and has attempted a more incisive treatment of relevant epigraphs, notably the Ghosuṇḍī, Besnagar and Mandasor inscriptions. The author takes this opportunity of expressing his thanks to Sir George Grierson, Professors Keith, Schrader and Garbe, Mr. A. Govindāchārya Svāmin and other scholars for having helped him with constructive criticism and suggestions. The revision of the text has necessitated a recasting of the Indexes. An attempt has been made to supply references that may be useful to the student.

But it is possible that there have been some important omissions. Errors, inaccuracies and misprints, both here and in the text itself, may also have escaped attention. For all these shortcomings the writer of these pages craves the indulgence of the reader.

UNIVERSITY OF CALCUTTA,
12th August, 1936. H. C. RAYCHAUDHURI.

ABBREVIATIONS

Ait. Āraṇyaka	... Aitareya Āraṇyaka.
Ait. Br.	... Aitareya Brāhmaṇa.
A. S. I.	... Archæological Survey of India (Annual Report).
As. Res.	... Asiatic Researches.
A. V.	... Atharva Veda Saṁhitā.
Bh. Purāṇa	... Bhāgavata Purāṇa.
Chh. Up.	... Chhāndogya Upanishad.
E. H. I.	... Early History of India, V. A. Smith.
E. H. D.	... Early History of the Dekkan, Sir R. G. Bhandarkar.
Ep. Ind.	... Epigraphia Indica.
G. E. I.	... The Great Epic of India, Hopkins.
Hist. Sans. Lit.	History of Sanskrit Literature, Macdonell.
I. H. Q.	... Indian Historical Quarterly.
Ind. Ant.	... Indian Antiquary.
Ind. Lit.	... Indian Literature, Weber.
J. R. A. S.	... Journal of the Royal Asiatic Society of Great Britain.
Kaush. Br.	... Kaushītaki Brāhmaṇa.
M. A. S. I.	... Memoirs of the Archæological Survey of India.
Mbh.	... Mahābhārata.

P. H. A. I. ... Political History of Ancient India (3rd edition).

R. I. { Religions of India, Barth.
Religions of India, Hopkins.

R. V. ... Ṛigveda Saṁhitā.

Saddharma ... Saddharmapuṇḍarīka.

Śat. Br. ... Śatapatha Brāhmaṇa.

S. B. E. ... Sacred Books of the East, Max Müller.

T. A. ... Taittirīya Āraṇyaka.

T. B. ... Taittirīya Brāhmaṇa.

CONTENTS

PAGE

Foreword 1

LECTURE I

Vaishṇavism and Vāsudeva 10

LECTURE II

The Life of Kṛishṇa Vāsudeva and the Early Progress of Bhāgavatism 62

LECTURE III

Bhāgavatism and the Non-Brāhmaṇical Creeds of Ancient India 119

LECTURE IV

Bhāgavatism in the Scythian, Gupta and Post-Gupta Periods 161

INDEXES

Bibliographic Index 197

General Index 206

Early History of the Vaishnava Sect

FOREWORD

"The most important branch of Indian history," says Vincent Smith, "is the history of her thought." "The soul of Hindu Civilisation," says C. N. Krishna Swami Aiyar, "is at once made out to be in the religious history of India." "The history of religion in India," he adds, "has a much larger meaning than it can have in connection with the civilisation of any other country or nationality." Hitherto the attention of Indologists has been mainly engrossed by the mighty religious movements associated with the names of Mahāvīra the Jina and Gautama the Buddha. Vaishṇavism and other orthodox Indian creeds have received but scant attention at the hands of scientific historians. The prevailing ignorance with regard to Vaishṇavism is reflected in such a widely read book of reference as Chambers's Twentieth Century Dictionary where Kṛishṇa is described as "a deity in later Hindu Mythology."

Whatever be the right kind of test in determining the importance of a religious system—the amount of the following, or the intrinsic worth of the system—Vaishṇavism must be regarded as one of the most important religions of India. It was the religion of Heliodoros, of the Gupta Emperors, of Rāmānuja, of Kavīra, of Chaitanya and of Tukārāma. It still counts as its votaries many among the teeming millions of India. It is the religion which produced the *Bhagavadgītā*, the songs of the Tamil *Āḻvārs*, the splendid *Padāvalīs* of mediæval Bengal, and the *Rāmacharitamānasa* of Tulasī Dās. If Sir George Grierson is right India owes the preservation of the ideas of *Bhakti* and *Prasāda* (loving faith and divine grace) to the Vaishṇavas. Any endeavour which is meant to throw light on the story of the rise and expansion of this important religion cannot but be of great use in reconstructing the history of our country. In his introduction to the *Sūtras* of Āpastamba[1] Dr. Bühler observes, "the earlier history of the Purāṇas, which as yet is a mystery, will only be cleared up when a real history of the orthodox Hindu sects, especially of the Śivites and Vishṇuites has been written." The writer of the following pages has tried to present the materials for a connected history of Vaishṇavism from the Vedic times to the age of the early Tamil *Āchāryas*

[1] P. xxix, n.

who laid the foundation of the *Śrī Vaishṇava* school of which the greatest exponent was Rāmānuja, the earliest of the celebrated mediæval Bhakti Reformers of India.

Valuable information regarding this faith has been supplied by several eminent scholars, Western as well as Indian, *e.g.*, Jones, Colebrooke, Wilson, Weber, Lorinser, Lassen, Muir, Bühler, Barth, Hopkins, Grierson, Garbe, Schrader, Niveditā, Macnicol, Keith, Vogel, Barnett, Hill, Carpenter, Eliot, Telang, Bhandarkar, Sukthankar, T. Rājagopāla Chariar, S. K. Aiyangar, Govindāchārya Swāmin, Dr. Seal, Bankimchandra, R. P. Chanda and others. The author has consulted their works and the following books and journals, *viz.*, the *Ṛig Veda*, the *Aitareya* and the *Śatapatha Brāhmaṇas*, the *Chhāndogya*, *Kaṭha* and *Śvetāśvatara Upanishads*, the *Taittirīya Āraṇyaka*, the *Nirukta* of Yāska, the *Ashṭādhyāyī* of *Pāṇini*, the *Mahābhāshya* of Patañjali, the *Sūtras* of Bodhāyaṇa, the *Mahābhārata* including the translations by P. C. Ray and M. N. Dutt, the *Matsya*, *Vāyu*, *Vishṇu* and *Bhāgavata Purāṇas*, the *Ahirbudhnya Saṁhitā*, the *Harsha-Charita* and the *Kādambarī* of Bāṇa, Saṅkara's Commentary on the *Sūtras* of Bādarāyaṇa, the *Buddhist Suttas* and *Jātakas*, the works of Aśvaghosha, the *Jaina Sūtras*, the *Journal of the Royal Asiatic Society*, the *Vienna Oriental Journal*, the *Indian Antiquary*, the *Epigraphia Indica*, the *Corpus*

Inscriptionum Indicarum, Macdonell and Keith's *Vedic Index*, Sorrensen's *Index of Names in the Mahābhārata* and other works references to which will be found in the following pages. In preparing these lectures the author has been mainly guided by the evidence of archæology, remembering the famous dictum of Colebrooke:[1] "In the scarcity of authentic materials for the ancient, and even for the modern, history of the Hindu race, importance is justly attached to all genuine monuments and especially inscriptions on stone and metal." He has also made use of literature to which an early date can be assigned, and which is comparatively free from late interpolations, *viz.*, (*i*) Pre-Buddhistic Vedic literature, (*ii*) ancient works to which a date in a definite epoch can be assigned, *e.g.*, the *Artha-Śāstra* attributed to Kauṭilya, the *Mahābhāshya* of Patañjali, the *Indika* of Megasthenes, the works of Aśvaghosha, etc., and (*iii*) works on Vāsudeva free from any Vaishṇava bias, *e.g.*, the *Ghata Jātaka* and the *Uttarādhyayana Sūtra*. The epics and the Purāṇas have been utilised very sparingly because of the numerous interpolations they contain and the uncertainty of their chronology.

In his first lecture the author has tried to draw a distinction between the worship of Urukrama-Vishṇu which is as old as the Ṛig Veda, and the

[1] *Essays*, Vol. II, p. 213.

Bhakti religion known as Vaishṇavism. He then tries to show that this *Bhakti* religion is not a plagiarism from Christianity, but owes its origin to Vāsudeva.

He next tries to prove the correctness of the tradition that the true Vāsudeva was Kṛishṇa, the famous prince of the Vṛishṇi family of Mathurā. In doing this he has attempted to demonstrate the unsoundness of the following theories, *viz.* :—

(1) That the true Vāsudeva, *i.e.*, the originator of Bhāgavatism, was not the Kshatriya prince Kṛishṇa, the son of Vasudeva.

(2) That Vāsudeva, though a Kshatriya prince, is not to be identified with Kṛishṇa.

(3) That Vāsudeva-Kṛishṇa was a solar deity.

(4) That Vāsudeva-Kṛishṇa was a tribal god.

(5) That Vāsudeva-Kṛishṇa was a vegetation deity.

In his second lecture the author proceeds to reconstruct the true history of the life of Vāsudeva-Kṛishṇa from such historical data as are available, and points out that Kṛishṇa came into contact with Solar worship, and the doctrines which he learnt from a Solar priest were the foundations on which the superstructure of Bhāgavatism was raised. Next follows the story of the spread of the new faith from its cradle in the valley of the Jumna. An attempt is made to show that the earlier Brāhmaṇical attitude towards the faith was one of hostility, but later on there was a combination between Brāhmaṇism and Bhāgavatism probably owing to the Buddhist propaganda of the Mauryas. As a result of this alliance Vāsudeva was identified with the Brāhmaṇic gods, Nārāyaṇa and Vishṇu.

In his third lecture the author discusses the question of the relation of Bhāgavatism to the following non-Brāhmaṇical creeds, *viz.*, Ājīvikism, Jainism, Buddhism and Christianity.

In his fourth lecture the author traces the fortunes of the Bhāgavata religion from the first century A.D. to the time of the Tamil *Āchāryas.* It is suggested that the Śaka and Kushān sovereigns of Northern India were generally not friendly towards the religion of Vāsudeva and this anti-Bhāgavata attitude may have brought the foreign kings into conflict with the Vaishṇava monarchs Chandra and the imperial Guptas. The Guptas did for Bhāgavatism what Aśoka had done for Buddhism. With the fall of the Guptas and the coming of the Huns Bhāgavatism lost its predominance in Northern India, but it flourished in the Tamil country and finally Rāmānuja and his followers restored it to the position it had held under the Guptas.

Bhāgavatism, like the religions of Mahāvīra and Buddha, was the expression of a natural reaction from the sacrifice-ridden religion of the Brāhmaṇic period. The earliest teachers of this faith, while refraining from an open denunciation of the *Vidhi Yajña* or the ordinary Vedic sacrifice, propounded a new doctrine which laid emphasis, among other things, on *Ahimsā*. *Ahimsā* is taught by the *guru* of Kṛishṇa Devakîputra in the *Chhāndogya Upanishad*.[1] Vishṇu, according to several Bhāgavata texts, appeared as four sons of *Dharma* and *Ahimsā*,[2] and his highest region (*param padam*) could only be reached by those who gave assurance of harmlessness to all creatures.[3]

Abhayam sarva bhutebhyo yo dadāti mahīpate
Sa gachchhati param sthānaṁ
Vishnoḥ padamanāmayam

A recent writer[4] considers the analogy suggested to Buddhism and Jainism to be 'superficial' and opines that "there was an intervening Upanishadic period in which the formal sacrificial religion of the Brāhmaṇas was being gradually replaced by a more intellectual theosophy, and that within this intellectual theosophy not only theistic but devotional tendencies were developing." It is, however, undeniable that Vāsudevism, like the religions of the Śākya sage and the Jñātrika reformer, originated amongst a free clan outside the Brāhmaṇical pale (*Vrātya*

1 iii. 17. 4.
2 Schrader, *Introduction to the Pañcarātra*, p. 44.
3 *Mahābhārata*, xi. 7. 25.
4 *Indian Historical Quarterly*, 1931, p. 97.

according to the *Mahābhārata*).[1] It laid emphasis on moral traits rather than ritualistic observances, glorified gods and heroes unknown to the Vedic pantheon, and centred round a personality that called forth the loving devotion of its followers which in due course fructified into *Bhakti*. Looked upon as heterodox by most of the people of the 'pale' where the literature on Brāhmaṇical ritual and theosophy was produced, the new faith nevertheless captured the imagination of the masses and produced a Holy Writ which was not the close preserve of a sacerdotal oligarchy but had a message even for the woman and the *Śūdra*.[2] As the first exponents of Bhāgavatism find mention in one of the earliest Upanishads it is hardly correct to say that the theistic and devotional tendencies noticeable in the younger Upanishads belong to a period which supervened between the Age of the Brāhmaṇas and the dawn of the Bhāgavata movement. It is rather the impact of new ideas radiating from the territories beyond "the fixed Middle Region" which leavened Brāhmaṇic thought and gave it a new orientation.

The new faith that developed on the banks of the Jumna finally coalesced with a few Brāhmaṇical and popular cults to form the great federation of religions known as Vaishṇavism. The agencies

[1] vii, 141, 15.

[2] The *Bhagavad-gītā*, ix, 32; *Brahma Purāṇa*, 178, 186.

employed in effecting this union were the following :—

(*i*) the *Vyūha* doctrine in virtue of which Vāsudevism united with Saṅkarshaṇa worship to form Bhāgavatism ;

(*ii*) the doctrine of *Avatāra* which effected a synthesis between Bhāgavatism and the cult of Vishṇu-Nārāyaṇa and gave birth to Vaishṇavism ;

(*iii*) the *Purusha-Prakṛiti* theory in virtue of which the cult of Śrī was engrafted on Vaishṇavism.

Just as the reaction against the old Vedic sacrifices gave birth to the intellectual movement of the Upanishadic Ṛishis and the religious movement of Kṛishṇa Vāsudeva, so the attempted revival of the *Karma-kāṇḍa* by the *Pūrva-Mīmāṁsā* school was followed by the neo-Vedāntic movement of Śaṅkarāchārya and the neo-Bhāgavatism of the Śrī Vaishṇava saints, the greatest amongst whom was Rāmānuja.

LECTURE I

VAISHṆAVISM AND VĀSUDEVA

Vaishṇavism is the name given to the Bhakti [1] religion which recognises Vishṇu, also called *Bhagavat* (the Blessed One), *Purushottama* (the Supreme Person), *Nārāyaṇa*, *Hari* as the sole God. He is defined as the Unborn (*Aja*), and the Eternal (*Śāśvata*). He is the Creator (*Dhātā*), the embodiment of Immortality (*Amṛitam*), the Father and the Mother and the Eternal Preceptor of the universe :—

Pitā mātā cha sarvasya
Jagataḥ śāśvato guruḥ.[2]

As occasion demands from time to time in His infinite grace (*prasāda*, *anugraha*) He Himself becomes incarnate to relieve the world from sin, or His followers from trouble. The most perfect incarnations (*avatāras*) are those of Rāma Dāśarathi and Kṛishṇa Vāsudeva.

1 The *Śāṇḍilyasūtram*, 1, 1, 2 defines *Bhakti* as *Parānurakti-rīśvare*, intense devotion to the Lord, *i.e.*, to God "conceived of as personal, a Saviour worthy of trust and ready to be gracious" (*cf.* Hill, *The Bhagavad Gītā*, p. 50; Mrinal Dasgupta, IHQ, 1930, pp. 315, 322 ff.).

2 Mbh. edited by P. Tarkaratna, xii, 334, 27.

Vishṇu worship is as old as the Ṛig Veda. Vishṇu is, as is well known, one of the manifestations of the sun. He envelops the earth on every side with rays of light (*mayukhaiḥ*).[1] He is often mentioned along with the Ādityas and is later reckoned as one of them.[2] He represents the sun in its daily and yearly course.[3] His fame rests on the three strides with which he crosses heaven :—

Idaṁ Vishṇur vichakrame tredhā nidadhe padam
samūlham asya pāṁsure
Trīṇipadā vichakrame Vishṇurgopā adābhyaḥ
ato dharmāṇi dhārayan.[4]

"Vishṇu strode over this (universe); in three places he planted his step : (the world, or his step was) enveloped in his dust. Vishṇu the unconquerable preserver, strode three steps, thereby maintaining fixed ordinances." [5]

" Three steps he made, the herdsman sure,
Vishṇu, and stepped across (the world)." [6]

"There can be little doubt," says Wilson, "that the three steps, here referred to, are the

1 *Ṛig Veda*, vii, 99, 3.

2 See Ṛig Veda, i, 90, 9; vii, 39, 5; x, 65, 1; 141-3; A. V. xi, 6, 2; Sat. Br. xiv, 1. 1, 10; Wilson's introduction to the *Ṛig Veda Saṁhitā*, Vol. I, p. xxviii and *Bhagavad Gītā*, x, 21.

3 Haug's translation of the *Aitareya Brāhmaṇa*, p. 1. n..

4 *Ṛig Veda*, i, 22, 17-18.

5 Muir, *Original Sanskrit Texts*, IV, 2nd ed., ch. 2.

Hopkins, *The Religions of India*, p. 57.

three periods of the sun's course—his rise, culmination and setting." It is expressly so stated by Aurṇavābha as explained by Durgāchārya in his commentary on the Nirukta.[1] Mr. Jayaswāl, however, thinks[2] that Aurṇavābha takes the verse "*idam Vishṇur vichakrame tredhā nidadhe padam*" in the sense that Vishṇu literally and physically in the past stepped over the earth, horizon and sky and "in ascending (he stepped) at the Vishṇupada on the Gayā peak." In the philosophy of the *Taittirīya Saṁhitā* the three places of Vishṇu are not the two points of the horizon and the zenith, but the earth, air and the sky.[3]

An ancient commentator, Śākapuni, understood the "three paces" to refer to the threefold manifestation of light as fire on earth, as lightning in the atmosphere and as the sun in the sky. Muir says that the explanation of Aruṇavābha (as quoted and elucidated by Durgāchārya) seems to satisfy best the idea of movement expressed in the description. On the other hand Keith points out that this interpretation is in flat contradiction with the references of the Vedas to the nature of the highest place of Vishṇu.[4]

1 Wilson's *Introduction to the Ṛig Veda Saṁhitā*, Vol. I, p. xxxiv; also p. 53. *Cf.* also Haug's *Ait. Br.*, p. 4, n. Muir, *Original Sanskrit Texts*, IV, vii.

2 *Ind. Ant.*, 1918, March, p. 84.

3 Hopkins, *The Religions of India*, p. 460.

4 Keith, *Religion and Philosophy of the Veda*, p. 108.

Colebrooke thought with Sāyaṇa that the taking of three steps might have formed the groundwork of the Paurāṇik legend of the Dwarf *Avatāra*. Wilson, however, remarked that it might have been suggestive of the fiction; but no allusion to the notion of *Avatāras* occurred in the Veda. As pointed out by Barnett [1] the old mythical feature of the three imperishable [2] steps of Vishṇu acquires a new spiritual meaning in later times and the 'three immortal steps' that lead to heaven are interpreted in a Besnagar inscription of the second century B. C. as denoting *dama, tyāga* and *apramāda,* self-control, renunciation and vigilance.

In one Ṛigvedic passage Vishṇu is called the germ of 'Ṛita,' *Ṛitasya garbham* ; [3] where 'Ṛita' may mean moral order or sacrifice. The idea is developed in later times. Vishṇu also figures in the Veda as a leader in battle. He is specially praised with Indra, the two being looked upon as masters of the world.[4] His greatness is inconceivable, and he is revered under the title *Śipivishṭa* [5] meaning 'clothed with rays of light' or 'bald.' He has three spaces, two called earthly, and one, the highest known only to himself and visible only to *Sūris*, apparently a class of

1 *Hindu Gods and Heroes*, p. 89.

2 *Ṛig Veda*, i, 154, 4.

3 i. 156, 3.

4 vi, 69; vii, 99.

5 vii, 100, 6.

specially favoured beings, " like an eye fixed in the sky."[1] Vishṇu's highest place (*parama pada*) which is a realm (*pāthas, vāstu*) beyond ordinary mortal ken,[2] which ' man apprehends not, nor can the soaring winged birds pursue,'[3] ' in which god-seeking men delight' and to which poets pray that people may go to enjoy felicity, may be plausibly described as a realm of departed spirits.[4] The later popularity of the deity, according to Hopkins, lies in the importance of his " highest place " being the home of departed spirits, where he himself dwells, inscrutable. The blessed abode (*paramam padam anāmayam*) of Vishṇu becomes the goal of spiritual endeavour in later ages.[5]

It is clear that Vishṇu was a great god even in the earliest Vedic times. But he was not regarded by anybody as the Sole God, or even as the greatest God. His inferiority to Indra appears even in the hymns devoted to his own glorification, and nothing better is said of him, in Ṛig Veda, i, 22, 19, than that "he is the worthy friend of Indra—*Indrasya yujyaḥ sakhā.*" He is also ordered about by Indra[6] :—

1 i, 155, 5; vii, 99 ; i, 22, 20.

2 vii, 99, 1.

3 *Ṛig Veda*, i, 155, 5.

4 i, 154, 5-6.

5 *Kaṭhopanishad*, i, 3, 9; Mbh. xi, 7. 25; *Gītā*, ii, 51.

6 iv, 18, 11; viii, 89, 12.

" His mother inquired of the mighty Indra, ' have these deities deserted thee, my son ?' Then Indra said, 'Vishṇu, my friend, (if thou) purpose slaying Vṛitra, exert thy greatest prowess.' "[1] Vishṇu strode his three steps by the energy of Indra.[2]

In the later Vedic literature the position of Vishṇu becomes more prominent. The Śatapatha Brāhmaṇa relates with great fullness of detail the legend regarding the 'three strides.' It further represents Vishṇu as the personification of sacrifice. We have already seen that as early as the Ṛigvedic age he was called the 'germ of the sacrifice.' "Vishṇu truly is the sacrifice, by striding (*vi-kram*) he obtained for the gods that all pervading power (*vikrānti*) which now belongs to them. By his first step he gained this same (earth), by the second this aerial expanse, and by his last (step) the sky. And this same pervading power Vishṇu, as the sacrifice, obtains by his strides for him (the sacrificer). For this reason he strides the Vishṇu-strides."[3]

The fourteenth *Kāṇḍa* of this Brāhmaṇa, at the beginning of its first part contains a legend of a contention among the gods, in which Vishṇu came off victorious, whence it became customary to

1 M. N. Dutt Śāstrī's translation of the Ṛig Veda Saṁhitā, p. 759.

2 *Ṛig Veda*, viii, 12, 27.

3 *Sat. Br.*, Part I, 9, 3, 9; Eggeling's translation of the Sat. Br., Part I, p. 268.

say, "Vishṇu is the most excellent of the gods." The gods sent forth ants to gnaw the bowstring of Vishṇu, who stood, resting his head on the end of the bow; the string snapping and springing upwards severed his head from his body. The head fell with (the sound) 'ghrin;' and on falling it became yonder sun (*Āditya*).[1]

The same legend with some variation recurs in a passage of the *Taittirīya Āraṇyaka*[2] and also in the *Pañchaviṁśa Brāhmaṇa*.[3]

We find the name Nārāyaṇa for the first time in the *Śatapatha Brāhmaṇa*, but it is not in any way connected with Vishṇu. It is in the *Taittirīya Āraṇyaka* that it is brought into direct relation to Vishṇu.

The prominent position held by Vishṇu in the Brāhmaṇic period is also manifest in the *Aitareya Brāhmaṇa* where he is said to occupy the highest place among the gods (*Agnirvaidevānāmavamo Vishṇuḥ paramaḥ*).[4] He is one of the '*Dīkshāpālau*'—the two guardians of the '*dīkshā*' or initiation.[5] He protects the defects in the sacrifice (from producing any evil consequences), while Varuṇa protects the fruits arising from its successful performance.[6] Vishṇu also figures in this work as a helper of Indra against the Asuras. "The

1 Eggeling's translation of the *Sat. Br.*, Part V, pp. 441-42; Weber's *History of Indian Literature*, pp. 126-27; Muir, *Original Sanskrit Texts*, IV, 123 ff.

2 v, 1. 3 vii, 5, 6. 4 Ait. Br., 1, 1.

5 i, 4. 6 iii, 38, Haug's translation, pp. 227-28.

Asuras after having been turned out, entered the *Śastra* of the *Achchhāvāka* (Priest). Indra said, "Who will join me, that we both turn out the Asuras from here?" Vishṇu answered, "I (will join you)." Indra and Vishṇu then turned the Asuras out.[1]

Although Vishṇu came to be looked upon by some as "the most excellent of the gods," he was, even now, far from being regarded by any section of the Aryan people as the One God. His pre-eminence among the gods is not always apparent and in a passage of the *Aitareya Brāhmaṇa* he is called *Devānām dvārapaḥ,*[2] the door-keeper of the gods, not a very complimentary epithet for the 'highest' among the gods.

Again, we have no evidence of the existence of a *Vaishṇava* sect in these early times. The sectarian name *Vaishṇava* is met with only in the latest portion of the *Mahābhārata* :[3]

> *Ashṭādaśa purāṇānām śravaṇād yat phalam bhavet*
> *Tat phalam samavāpnoti Vaishṇavonātra saṁśayaḥ.*

"(By listening to the *Bhārata*) a *Vaishṇava* acquires that merit which is gained by listening to the eighteen *Purāṇas*. There is no doubt about that."

1 iii. 50; Haug's translation, p. 254.

2 i, 30.

3 xviii, 6, 97.

The exact date of this portion of the Great Epic is, no doubt, uncertain. But from numismatic evidence it seems probable that the epithet "*Parama Vaishṇava*" came into general use only from about the fifth century A.D.[1] We should also note another important fact, namely, that there is very little inner connection between Vedic and Brāhmaṇic Vishṇu-worship and the Bhakti religion we call Vaishṇavism. The idea of a God of Grace, the doctrine of Bhakti—these are the fundamental tenets of the religion termed Vaishṇavism. But they are not very conspicuous in Vedic and Brāhmaṇic Vishṇu-worship. Vishṇu in the Brāhmaṇic texts is more intimately connected with '*yajña*' (sacrifice) than with *Bhakti* or *Prasāda*. It is in the hymns addressed to Varuṇa, and not in those addressed to Vishṇu, that we find a feeling which bears some resemblance to the Vaishṇava *Bhakti*.[2]

Dr. Macnicol, indeed, sees some hints in the *Brāhmaṇa* literature of the progress which Vishṇu was making behind the screen of Brāhmaṇic ritual, to the position he has held so long as the Supreme God of those in India whose hearts are

1 *Cf.* the "Traikuṭaka" coins mentioning "*Parama-Vaishṇava* Śrī-Mahārāja Dahrasena" and "*Parama-Vaishṇava* Śrī-Mahārāja Vyāghra (Sena)," Rapson, *Catalogue of the Coins of the Andhra Dynasty*, etc., pp. 198, 202.

2 Ind. Ant., 1908, p. 259; J.R.A.S., 1915, p. 834; Macnicol's *Indian Theism*, p. 10; Hill, the *Bhagavadgītā*, p. 50.

filled with Bhakti.[1] But these hints are extremely dubious. Dr. Keith rightly observes[2] "That the Brāhmaṇas treat Vishṇu as identical with the sacrifice and ask him to make good its defects do not show that he was 'on his way to his place as the God of the worship of men's hearts,' or 'was recognised in his aspect of grace as a saviour.'" If the Vedic or Brāhmaṇic accounts of Vishṇu-worship do not furnish any clue to the origin of Vaishṇavism as we know it, what is its source ?

In the opinion of several scholars this Bhakti Religion was of foreign origin, and was preached in India for the first time by Rāmānuja. "There has been considerable mis-impression," says S. Krishnaswami Aiyangar[3] "that the Vaishṇava movement originated in Rāmānuja....On the basis of this mis-impression, theories have been built up time and again that the characteristic features of the special teachings of Rāmānuja have been borrowed from Christianity." Dr. Keith observes :[4] "The first great theistic movement of India is that of Rāmānuja...........But precisely at this point we are met with the fact that Christian religious influences are possible and even probable."

Mr. Aiyangar rightly considers the hypothesis of a plagiarism from Christianity to be an error

1 *Indian Theism*, p. 30.
2 J.R.A.S., 1915, p. 839.
3 *Sri Rāmānujāchārya*, p. 2.
4 J.R.A.S., 1915, pp. 836-37.

which arises from not giving due weight to the indebtedness of Rāmānuja to those Tamil Saints that had gone before him ere he came into the world. The Tamil Saints to whom Mr. Aiyangar refers are the *Āchāryas* Nāthamuni and Ālvandār (Yāmunāchārya) and their precursors the *Āḻvārs*.[1]

Rāmānuja begins his *Vedārtha Saṁgraha* as well as his commentary on the *Bhagavadgītā* by paying his tribute of respect to Yāmunāchārya. A work of the latter, the *Siddhitraya*, is frequently quoted in Rāmānuja's works, and Rāmānuja generally follows the same lines of argument as we find in Yāmuna's work.[2] Yāmunāchārya in his turn was the spiritual successor of his grandfather Nāthamuni, the author of the *Nyāya Tattva* "an elaborate treatise covering the whole field of philosophy from the point of view of the Rāmānuja school."[3] Nāthamuni again got his inspiration from the songs of the *Āḻvārs*, especially from those of Saint Śaṭakopa.[4] The *Āḻvārs* were saints or *Bhaktas* of various castes, who by their Tamil songs inculcated *Bhakti* and Kṛishṇa-worship mainly.[5] The *Bhagavadgītā* was well known to them and the *Bhāgavata* in some form also. "It

1 *Srī-Rāmānujāchārya*, p. 4.

2 V. A. Sukhtankar's "*Teachings of Vedānta according to Rāmānuja*," *The Vienna Oriental Journal*, Vol. 22, 1908, pp. 121-22.

3 T. Rājagopāla Chariar's "*The Vaishṇavite Reformers of India*," p. 4.

4 *Op. cit.*, pp. 2-3.

5 *Op. cit.*, p. 138.

seems reasonable to conclude," says Mr. T. Rājagopāla Chariar, "that these *Āḷvārs* or the earlier of them were offshoots of the northern Bhāgavatas." Colebrooke gives an account of the Bhāgavatas in his *Miscellaneous Essays*.[1] The synonymy of the *Bhāgavata* sect is thus given in the *Pādma Tantra*, one of the 108 *Tantras* or *Saṁhitās* which constitute the sacred canon of an important section of *Vaishṇavas* :—

Sūris Suhṛid Bhāgavatas Sātvataḥ Pañchakāla-vit
Ekāntikas Tanmayaś cha Pañcharātrika ityapi.[2]

The Bhāgavata, Sātvata, Ekāntika or Pañcharātra religion is referred to in the *Nārāyaṇīya* section of the *Sāntiparva* and the *Viśvopākhyāna* of the *Bhīshma-parva* of the *Mahābhārata* :—

"*Yadā Bhāgavato ' tyarthamāsīdrājā mahān Vasuḥ.*"[3]

"*Sātvatam vidhimāsthāya prāksūryamukha-niḥsṛitam.*"[4]

"*Nūnam Ekāntadharmo'yam śreshṭho Nārāyaṇapriyaḥ.*"[5]

"*Pañcharātra vidomukhyāstasya gehemahātmanaḥ*"[6]

Dvāparasya yugasyānte ādau Kaliyugasyacha Sātvatam Vidhimāsthāya gītaḥ Saṅkarshaṇenavai.[7]

1 Vol. I, pp. 437-43.
2 J.R.A.S., 1911, p. 935.
3 Mbh., xii, 337, 1.
4 Mbh., xii, 335, 19.
5 Mbh., xii, 348, 4.
6 Mbh., xii, 235, 25.
7 Mbh., vi, 66, 40.

According to the *Mahābhārata*[1] this religion was obtained by Nārada from Nārāyaṇa Himself. "It has once before been concisely told in the *Harigītā* (that is, the *Bhagavadgītā*)." In another passage, in reply to Janamejaya's question "who taught it first?" Vaiśampāyana says "it was told by the Adorable Himself to Arjuna" (*i.e.*, in the *Bhagavadgītā*).[2]

The date of the *Bhagavadgītā*, of the *Viśvopākhyāna* or of the *Nārāyaṇīya* is uncertain, but we have epigraphic evidence of the existence of the *Bhāgavata* or *Bhakti* school long before the beginning of the Christian era.[3]

A Besnagar inscription[4] of the second century B.C. mentions the erection of a flagstaff with an image of Garuḍa at the top in honour of Vāsudeva by Heliodora, an ambassador of the Greek king Antialkidas, who was a *Bhāgavata*. Another epigraph of a slightly later date, evidently from Besnagar, records the erection of a Garuḍa column "of the excellent temple (*Prāsādottama*) of the *Bhagavat*" by Gautamîputra.........a *Bhāgavata*, in the twelfth year after the installation of the

1 xii, 346, 10-11.

2 Mbh., xii, 348, 6-8.

3 See *The Indian Antiquary*, 1912, p. 13; R. P. Chanda, *Archæology and Vaishṇava Tradition*, *Memoirs of the Archæological Survey of India*, No. 5.

4 Lüders, Ins. No. 669 (*Epigraphia Indica*, Vol. X, Appendix), Vogel, *ASI*, 1908-9, 126-29. Besnagar, ancient Vidiśā, is in Eastern Malwa.

Great King Bhāgavata. A third monument of about the same date has been discovered in the same locality in which Mr. Chanda recognises the remnant of a *Makaradhvaja* or a "crocodile column" which is the emblem of Pradyumna, the son of Vāsudeva. The Ghosūṇḍī Inscription,[1] probably engraved a little earlier, speaks of a *pūjā* stone wall for the worship of Bhagavat Saṅkarshaṇa and Vāsudeva. Another inscription probably of the first century B.C. existing at Nānāghāṭ[2] contains an adoration of Saṅkarshaṇa and Vāsudeva.[3]

These epigraphic records show clearly that the *Bhāgavatas* were the *Bhaktas* of Vāsudeva. This fact enables us to trace back the existence of the sect to the age of Pāṇini for we must recognise in the *Vāsudevakas* of that grammarian the forerunners of the *Bhāgavatas* of the second century B.C.

In the *sūtra*, iv, 3, 95, Pāṇini says that an affix comes after a word in the first case in construction in the sense of "this is his object of *Bhakti*." Then in a succeeding *sūtra*, iv, 3, 98, he says that

[1] Lüders, Ins. No. 6; *Ind. Ant.*, 1932, 203 ff.; Ghosuṇḍî is about 4 miles from Nagari in the Udayapura State, Rājputāna.

[2] Lüders, Ins. No. 1112; Nānāghāṭ is in the Deccan.

[3] In connection with the antiquity of the cult of Kṛishṇa (Vāsudeva) mention may be made of a story recorded by Zenob, a Syrian who flourished about 304 A.D., regarding the erection of a temple to *Giṣane* (Kṛishṇa?) by the sons of certain Indian chiefs who had fled westwards with their clan and found shelter in Armenia (149-127 B.C.)—see Kennedy, *The Indians in Armenia*, JRAS, 1904, 309 ff.

the affix '*Vun*' comes in the sense of "this is his object of *Bhakti*" after the words Vāsudeva and Arjuna. Thus Vāsudevaka = a person the object of whose *Bhakti* is Vāsudeva. To this word we may compare the word Gotamaka = a follower of Gotama.[1]

It is agreed on all hands that Pāṇini flourished before Patañjali [2] who wrote the great commentary (*Mahābhāshya*) on his sūtras apparently in the second century B.C.

But the exact date of this prince of grammarians is uncertain. According to Hopkins [3] "no evidence has yet been brought forward to show conclusively that Pāṇini lived before the third century B.C." Böhtlingk places him in the fourth century B.C. and his view is accepted by Macdonell,[4] Keith and many other western scholars; while Sir R. G. Bhandarkar says that "Pāṇini must have flourished in the beginning of the seventh century B.C. if not earlier still." [5]

As the question of Pāṇini's date is important for determining the antiquity of the Bhāgavata religion it will not be quite out of place to state our own views on the subject.

1 Rhys Davids, *Dialogues of the Buddha*, I, pp. 220-222; *Buddhist India*, p. 145.

2 For references see V. A. Smith's E.H.I., 3rd Edition, p. 214.

3 *The Great Epic of India*, p. 391.

4 *Sanskrit Literature*, p. 17.

5 E. H. D., p. 8.

Pāṇini lived not only before Patañjali, but also before Kātyāyana who wrote the *Vārttikas* (explanatory and supplementary rules) on his grammar, and who was himself a predecessor of Patañjali. This fact forbids the acceptance of the theory of Hopkins that Pāṇini lived in the third century B.C.; for that would leave an interval of considerably less than a century between Kātyāyana and Patañjali. The actual interval between these two grammarians cannot be so short because Sir R. G. Bhandarkar points out that Patañjali notices variant readings of Kātyāyana's *Vārttikas* as found in the texts used by the schools of the Bhāradvājīyas, Saunāgas and others.

Böhtlingk's theory rests upon a story in the *Kathāsaritsāgara*, a collection of popular tales belonging to the eleventh century A.D., where Pāṇini is said to have been the disciple of one Varsha, who lived at Pāṭaliputra in the reign of King Nanda. But as Weber points out[1] the authority of such a work is extremely questionable in reference to a period fifteen centuries earlier. Moreover, the work makes Kātyāyana a contemporary of Pāṇini.[2] But as Goldstücker points out the two grammarians really belonged to two different periods of Hindu antiquity.[3] The assertion is also contradicted by a statement of Kātyāyana

1 *Ind. Lit.*, p. 217.

2 See Goldstücker's *Pāṇini, His place in Sanskrit Literature*, p. 61.

3 *Op. cit.*, p. 93.

himself. A rule of Pāṇini, iv, 3, 105, teaches us that the names of *Brāhmaṇas* and *Kalpas* are formed by adding the affix "*ṇini*" to the proper names of the personage who proclaims them, provided that such a personage is an *old* authority. As the Brāhmaṇas proclaimed by Yājñavalkya are not formed by the affix "*ṇini*" it is clear that Pāṇini did not include Yājñavalkya among the old authorities.[1]

To Pāṇini's rule Kātyāyana adds a *Vārttika* "among the *Brāhmaṇas* and *Kalpas* which are proclaimed by an *old* one there is an exception in reference to Yājñavalkya and so on, on account of the contemporaneousness namely, of these latter *Brāhmaṇas*, with the old *Brāhmaṇas* spoken of by Pāṇini."[2]

Thus works (*e.g.*, the *Brāhmaṇas* proclaimed by Yājñavalkya) which Pāṇini did not include among the "*purāṇaprokta*" *Brāhmaṇas* came to be considered by Kātyāyana to be as old as those which were old to Pāṇini. The two grammarians, therefore, could not have been contemporaries.

Kātyāyana's date, fourth century B.C., may now be relied upon. This date does not solely depend on 'the ghost story' of the *Kathā-sarit-sāgara*[3] but follows from the ascertained date of

1 Goldstücker, *Pāṇini*, p. 101.

2 *Op. cit.*, p. 105.

3 As Dr. R. L. Mitra says in his Introduction to the *Aitareya Āraṇyaka*,

Patañjali.[1] The interval of two centuries between Kātyāyana and Patañjali will not appear too long when we remember that the grammarians of the schools of the *Bhāradvājīyas* and *Saunāgas, Kuṇaravāḍava, Saurya Bhāgavat* and *Kuṇi* lived before Patañjali and after Kātyāyana since all their *Vārttikas* or remarks, recorded by Patañjali, are criticisms on, and emendations of, the *Vārttikas* of Kātyāyana.[2]

Pāṇini, therefore, lived before the fourth century B.C. But it is difficult to accept the statement of Sir R. G. Bhandarkar that he cannot be placed later than the seventh century B.C. A tradition recorded in the *Kāvya-Mīmāṁsā*, dated about the ninth century A.D., says that the great grammarian won fame in the great centre of learning at Pāṭaliputra, a city founded after the death of the Buddha. Pāṇini knows not merely "the three *saṁhitās* of the *Ṛik, Sāman* and *Black Yajus*," as contended by Goldstücker,[3] but also *Brāhmaṇas* and *Kalpas*[4] and refers to *Sūtrakāras*.[5] He also mentions the *Mahābhārata*[6] which is not recognised in any Sanskrit literary work till after the end of the *Brāhmaṇa* period, and only in the *Grihya Sūtras*. Pāṇini's date must, therefore, fall in the age of the latest sūtras.

1 E.H.D., p. 7; E.H.I., 3rd edition, p. 451, n.

2 Goldstücker, *Pāṇini*, 1914, p. 68.

3 *Pāṇini*, p. 108.

4 iv, 3, 105.

5 iii, 2, 23.

6 vi. 2, 38.

The most important chronological datum is furnished by the mention of *Yavana*.[1] *Yavana*, or *Yona* was a term used in ancient India to denote the Greeks. In Aśoka's Rock Edict XIII Antiochos is called a *Yonarāja*. In the Besnagar Pillar Inscription Heliodoros, the ambassador of Antialkidas, is called a *Yonadūta*. We know from the cuneiform inscriptions of the Achaemenian Kings of Persia that they had no other name for the Greeks but *Ya-u-na*.[2] This Persian form of the name *Yavana* was not unknown to the Hindus :—

Uttarāpathajanmānaḥ kīrtayishyāmi tānapi
Yauna Kāmboja Gāndhārāḥ Kirātā Barbaraiḥ saha.[3]

It is a desperate resort to imagine that this well-known ethnic term really means non-Greeks.[4] Pāṇini in his *Sūtra* iv, 1, 49, explains the formation of the word *Yavanāni*—to which, according to the *Vārttika*, the word '*lipi*,' writing, must be supplied, and which therefore signifies "the writing of the *Yavanas* or Greeks," and not "the

1 iv, 1, 49.

2 *Ind. Ant.*, 1875, p. 245.

3 Mbh., xii, 207, 43.

4 The theory that "the term Yavana does not indicate Greek nationality" has recently been revived by some scholars (*Indian Culture*, Vol. I, No. 3, 1935, p 356) and attention is invited to "the apparent Iranian nationality" of the Yavana Tushāspha of the Junāgaḍh Inscription of Rudradāman. It is forgotten that the *Yavanas* are sharply distinguished from the *Kambojas* by Aśoka, from the *Palhavas* by Queen

writing of the Persians," or "the cuneiform writing.[1] The employment by the Indians of a special term and affix to denote the Greek writing could only have arisen after long acquaintance with the *Yavanas* and their alphabet. Such a prolonged intercourse between the Indians and the Greeks was not in my opinion possible in the seventh century B.C. when the empires of Assyria and Media intervened between India and Hellas, but was possible, and even probable after the Achaemenian conquest of Gandhāra, the native land of Pāṇini, for the Persian empire formed a link which connected India with Greece, and Greek mercenaries and Greek officials were largely employed by the Persian Kings and Satraps.[2]

Pāṇini therefore, in all probability, lived after the Persian conquest of Gandhāra in the latter half of the sixth century B.C., but before the

Gotamī Balasirī and the Great Satrap Rudradāman and from the *Pārasīkas* by the poets of the *Mahābhārata* and by Viśākha-datta, the author of the *Mudrā-rākshasa* (*Act 2,—Astitāvachchhaka-Yavana-Kirāta-Kāmboja-Pārasīka-Vālhika-prabhṛitibhih...............samantāduparuddhaṁ Kusumapuram*). If Tushāspha was an Iranian, it may with equal reason be argued that Vāsudeva, the successor of Huvishka, and Suviśākha, the Parthian Governor of Rudradāman, were native Hindus of India. Kālidāsa (*Raghuvaṁsa*, IV, 60 ff.) has been relied on by some to establish the equation Yavana=Pārasīka. But the *Yavanīs* of *Raghu*, IV, 61, have been mentioned in connection with the *land-route* (*Sthala-vartma*) *leading to* the "*western*" realm which was the country of the Persians. Raghu's army, avoiding the sea-route, had suddenly overspread the *Yavana* country (apparently in the Kābul valley) like a mass of clouds and thence proceeded to the land of the *śmaśrula* westerners, *i.e*, the Persians.

1 Goldstücker, *Pāṇini*, 1914, p. 12.

2 Rapson, *Ancient India*, p. 87.

fourth century B.C. With a date in the fifth century B.C. all the evidence accommodates itself. With such a date accords the fact that Pāṇini knows the Persians as a warlike people[1] but, unlike later grammarians, never alludes to the Yavanas or Śakas as fighting races. The interval of a century between Pāṇini and Kātyāyana is not too short in view of the fact that "the oldest author on record who wrote on Pāṇini was Kātyāyana."[2]

Since Pāṇini probably flourished in the fifth century B.C. the *Bhāgavata* (*Vāsudevaka*) sect must have arisen before that time. We learn from the *Sūtras*, iv, 3, 95 and iv, 3, 98, that the new faith was even in the fifth century B.C. a religion of *Bhakti*. It has recently been suggested by Mr. Umeshchandra Bhaṭṭāchārya[3] that *Bhakti* in rules iv, 3, 95 ff., can hardly mean religious adoration as it is used in reference to even cakes (*apūpa*). He asks "is not fondness (*anurakti*) a possible meaning in the rules we are considering?" But *anurakti* for one who, as we shall see further on, is identified with Vishṇu-Nārāyaṇa as early as the *Taittirīya Āraṇyaka* and receives the epithets *Bhagavat* and *Devadeva* in records of the second century B.C., is hardly distinguishable from *Bhakti* in the religious sense as defined by

1 v 3, 117.

2 Goldstücker, *Pāṇini*, 1914, p. 90.

3 IHQ, 1925, 483-9.

Śāṇḍilya. Another writer suggests that *Bhakti* in the rules of Pāṇini is political *Bhakti* because there is no evidence that Arjuna, whose name is coupled with that of Vāsudeva in rule iv, 3, 98, was deified. It is, however, well-known that already in the great epic Arjuna is regarded as an incarnation of Nara and is called *Bhaktānukampī* like unto Mahendra and Varuṇa.[1] In the *Vishvaksena Saṁhitā* Arjuna is classed with Brahman, Śiva and a few others among the secondary *Avatāras* of Vishṇu.[2]

We have seen that the religion preached by Rāmānuja and professed by the Ālvārs existed before the Christian era, and that its votaries were called *Bhāgavatas* or *Vāsudevakas*, *i.e.*, the *Bhaktas* or followers of Vāsudeva. Vāsudeva is thus the fountain-head of Vaishṇavism. No doubt under the comprehensive designation of Vaishṇavism are included a number of sectaries who recognise other personages than Vāsudeva as their Saviour. The most important of these are the followers of Rāmānanda and Kavīra. But the vast majority of the Vaishṇavas are still Vāsudevites and even those who pay exclusive devotion to Rāma cannot trace the origin of their doctrine to any other source than Rāmānuja who, as we have seen, owes his tenets to the earlier *Āchāryas* and

1 Mbh., iii, 45, 12; 47, 10-14.

2 Schrader, *Introduction to the Pāñcarātra*, p. 48.

Āḷvārs, who in their turn were offshoots from the *Bhāgavatas* or *Vāsudevakas* of Northern India mentioned in the inscriptions discovered at Besnagar and Ghosūṇḍī and also in the *Ashṭādhyāyī* of that prince of grammarians, Pāṇini.

We have little authentic information regarding Vāsudeva, round whom the *Bhāgavata* movement centred. The name Vāsudeva occurs once in the Vedic literature, *viz.*, in a passage of the tenth Prapāṭhaka of the Taittirīya Āraṇyaka—*Nārāyaṇāya vidmahe Vāsudevāya dhīmahi tanno Vishṇuḥ prachodayāt.* Here Vāsudeva is a name of Vishṇu. But the last book of the Taittirīya Āraṇyaka is a comparatively late work.[1] It is described as *khilarūpa* or supplementary. Vishṇu does not receive the name 'Vāsudeva' in any of the *Saṁhitās, Brāhmaṇas* or *classical Upanishads.*

In the *Bhagavadgītā* "which contains probably the oldest dogmatic exposition we possess of Vishṇuism"[2] and which is recognised as an *Upanishad* by the Hindus, Vāsudeva is said to have been a scion of the Vṛishṇi family :—

Vṛishṇinām Vāsudevo'smi Pāṇḍavānām
Dhanañjayaḥ.

The Vṛishṇi origin of Vāsudeva is apparently hinted at in a Mora stone slab inscription of the time of the Great Satrap Rājuvula (first century

1 Dr. R. L. Mitra's Introduction to the T. A., p. 8.

2 Barth, *The Religions of India*, p. 191 ; *cf.* also Mbh., xii, 348,6-8.

A.D.).[1] The Vṛishṇis are mentioned in the *Ashṭādhyāyī* of Pāṇini[2] and in the *Arthaśāstra* attributed to Kauṭilya.[3] Scions of the family are apparently mentioned in the *Taittirīya Saṁhitā*,[4] the *Taittirīya Brāhmaṇa*,[5] the *Śatapatha Brāhmaṇa*[6] and the *Jaiminīya Upanishad Brāhmaṇa*.[7]

The *Ghata Jātaka*[8] gives the Buddhist version of the story of Vāsudeva just as the *Daśaratha Jātaka* gives the Buddhist version of the legend of Rāma. It describes Vāsudeva as a scion of the royal family of "Upper Madhurā"[9] but does not give the name of the family. But it is not difficult to find out that the Vṛishṇi family is meant. The *Jātaka* says that the family of Vāsudeva perished for their irreverent conduct towards Kaṇhadīpāyana.[10] The *Kauṭilīya Artha-śāstra* refers to this incident but substitutes "the corporation of the Vṛishṇis" for the family of Vāsudeva :—

"Whoever has not his organs of sense under his control, will soon perish.........Vātāpi in his attempt under the influence of overjoy to attack Agastya, as well as the corporation of the Vṛishṇis in their attempt against Dvaipāyana."[11]

1 *Memoirs of the Archaeological Survey of India*, No. 5, 166.

2 iv, 1, 114.

3 R. Shama Sastry's translation, p. 13.

4 iii, 11, 9, 3.

5 iii, 10, 9, 15.

6 iii, 1, 1, 4.

7 i, 6, 1.

8 The Jātakas, Cowell's edition, Vol. IV, p. 50.

9 Pp. 50-51.

10 Pp. 55-56.

11 R. Shama Sastry's translation of Kauṭilya's Arthaśāstra, pp. 12-13.

The Jaina *Uttarādhyayana Sūtra,* Lecture XXII, confirms the statement of the *Gītā* and the *Jātaka* that Vāsudeva was a Kshatriya Prince.

The *Mahābhārata,* the great storehouse of Hindu tradition, usually takes Vāsudeva to mean "the son of Vasudeva." [1] But in certain passages a different etymology is given.

Vasanāt sarvabhūtānām vasutvāddevayonitaḥ
Vāsudevastato vedyo bṛihattvād Vishṇuruchyate.[2]

"He is called Vāsudeva in consequence of his enveloping all creatures with the screen of illusion, or of his glorious splendour, or of his being the support and resting place of the gods."

Chhādayāmi jagad viśvam bhūtvā sūrya ivāmśubhiḥ
Sarvabhūtādhivāsaścha Vāsudevastatohyaham.[3]

"Assuming the form of the Sun I cover the universe with my rays. And because I am the home of all creatures, therefore, am I called by the name of Vāsudeva."

The *Mahābhārata* knows a false Vāsudeva as well as the true Vāsudeva. The false Vāsudeva was a king of the Pauṇḍras.[4] The true Vāsudeva was Kṛishṇa, the famous prince of the *Yādava, Vṛishṇi* or *Sātvata* family of Mathurā. It is written in the *Śāntiparva*[5] that the *Sātvata* or

1 *Cf.* Mbh., iii, 14, 8.
2 Mbh., v, 70, 3.
3 Mbh., xii, 341, 41.
4 Mbh., i, 186, 12; ii, 14, 20; etc.
5 Mbh., xii, 348, 6-8.

Bhāgavata Dharma was first taught by Kṛishṇa Vāsudeva to Arjuna :—

Samupoḍheshvanīkeshu Kuru Pāṇḍavayormṛidhe
Arjune vimanaske cha gītā Bhagavatā svyam.[1]

"It was sung by the Blessed One Himself when armies were drawn up for battle in the Kuru-Pāṇḍava war and Arjuna became dispirited."

This fact forbids the acceptance of the theory of Mr. A. Govindāchārya Svāmin that the *Bhāgavata Śāstra* was "not originated by Vāsudeva—the son of Vasudeva—*i.e.*, Kṛishṇa,"[2] because forsooth, the word Vāsudeva also means "He who permeates all" and the *Pādmatantra* distinguishes between the two Vāsudevas. The name *Sātvata Dharma* applied to the Bhāgavata religion also shows that it originated in the *Sātvata* prince Vāsudeva. The association of Vāsudeva with Saṅkarshaṇa in the Bhāgavata inscriptions of the first and second centuries B.C. also proves that Kṛishṇa, the brother of Saṅkarshaṇa (*Saṅkarshaṇāṇuja*),[3] was the real Vāsudeva worshipped by the early Bhāgavatas.

According to Sir R. G. Bhandarkar, Vāsudeva and Kṛishṇa were originally names of distinct individuals. In the opinion of that great scholar Vāsudeva was a Kshatriya belonging to the Yādava, Vṛishṇi or Sātvata race who founded a

[1] Mbh., xii, 348, 8.
[2] J. R. A. S., 1911, p. 936.
[3] Mbh., ii, 79, 23.

theistic system. Later on "he was identified with Kṛishṇa whose name had been handed down as that of a holy seer." [1]

Nobody will deny the existence of several "holy seers" bearing the name of Kṛishṇa who were quite distinct from Vāsudeva of the Vṛishṇi race. Such were Kṛishṇa, the father of Viśvakāya,[2] Kṛishṇa Āṅgirasa,[3] Kṛishṇa Hārita[4] and Kaṇha, the mighty seer mentioned in the *Ambaṭṭha sutta*.[5] But it is impossible to accept the statement that Kṛishṇa whom epic tradition identifies with Vāsudeva was originally an altogether different individual. On the contrary all available evidence, Hindu, Buddhist and Greek, points to the correctness of the identity; and we agree with Keith when he says that "the separation of Vāsudeva and Kṛṣṇa as two entities it is impossible to justify." [6]

We learn from Patañjali that the event of the death of Kaṁsa at the hands of Kṛishṇa was

1 *Ind. Ant.*, 1912, p. 13.

2 *Ṛig Veda*, i, 116, 23; i, 117, 7.

The identification of Kṛishṇa who lived on the banks of the Aṁsumatī (*Ṛig Veda*, VIII, 96, 13f) with his epic and Purāṇic namesake (P. T. Srinivāsa Iyengar, *Life in Ancient India*, pp. 131ff; Radhakrishnan, *The Heart of Hindusthan*, p. 51; *Indian Philosophy*, Vol. I, p. 493) is implausible. The Aṁsumatī is not the Jumna as stated by Iyengar but a river in the Kuru country (Macdonell, *The Bṛihad-devatā*, part II, p. 238).

3 Kaush. Br., xxx, 9.

4 Ait. Āraṇyaka. iii, 2, 6.

5 Rhys Davids, Dialogues of the Buddha, I, p. 118.

6 J. R. A. S., 1915, p. 840.

in his age believed to have occurred in the remote past. He says "*chirahate Kaṁse*" which means that Kaṁsa's death occurred at a very remote time. That Kṛishṇa was the name of the slayer is evident from the following statements found in the *Mahābhāshya* :—

"*Prahārādriśyante Kaṁsasyacha Kṛishṇasyacha.*"
"*Asādhur mātule Kṛishṇaḥ.*"

But in another place it is said that "in the days of yore Vāsudeva killed Kaṁsa"—*Jaghāna Kaṁsam kila Vāsudevaḥ*. It is thus clear that from the remotest times, from the period when the feud between Kaṁsa and his nephew was believed to have taken place, an age which was considered to be an ancient one even by Patañjali, Kṛishṇa and Vāsudeva were considered to be names of one and the same individual—the slayer of Kaṁsa. Sir R. G. Bhandarkar points out[1] that in Kielhorn's edition of the *Mahābhāshya* the name 'Vāsudeva' takes the place of Kṛishṇa in one passage; but then, from no manuscript is the name Kṛishṇa entirely absent. The frequency of the name 'Vāsudeva' may be due to the fact which he has himself proved that it was the proper name, while 'Kṛishṇa' was the *Gotra* name.[2]

1 *Vaiṣṇavism*, etc., p. 10.
2 Pp. 10, 12.

In the *Ghata-Jātaka* Vāsudeva receives the epithet "Kaṇha" that is, Kṛishṇa :—

"Just then a courtier named Rohiṇeyya, went into the presence of King Vāsudeva, and opened a conversation with him by reciting the first stanza :

"*Black Kaṇha, rise! why close the eyes to sleep? why lying there?*

Thine own brother—see the winds away his wit do bear,

Away his wisdom! Ghata raves, thou of the long black hair!" [1]

The Greek writers, Megasthenes and Arrian, mention Herakles as one held in special honour by the Sourasenoi, an Indian tribe who possessed two large cities Methora and Kleisobora.[2] Bhandarkar identifies the Sourasenoi with the Sātvatas and Herakles with Vāsudeva. According to Lassen, McCrindle and Hopkins, Methora and Kleisobora are Mathurā and Kṛishṇapura.[3] Now, Megasthenes lived full two centuries before Patañjali. The name of the second city (Kṛishṇapura) mentioned by him is a certain indication of the early and inseparable connection of Kṛishṇa with the Sourasenoi (Śūrasenas) or Sātvatas.

1 Cowell's *Jātaka*, Vol. IV, p. 54.

2 McCrindle, Ancient India as described by Megasthenes and Arrian, p. 201.

3 McCrindle's Megasthenes and Arrian, p. 140, n.; Ind. Ant., 1876, p. 334; Hopkins, The Religions of India, p. 459.

In the *Chhāndogya Upanishad*[1] Kṛishṇa learns the same doctrines—*tapodānamārjjavam ahiṁsā satyavachanam*—which Vāsudeva teaches in the *Gītā*.[2]

The rank growth of legend which has clustered round the name of Kṛishṇa Vāsudeva reminds us of the extravagant tales which obscure the genuine history of Kapila, of Buddha, and of Aśoka. The Kṛishṇa stories may not all be either fiction or myth ; but they are no better suited to serve as the foundation of sober history than the tales of the *Bhāgavata Purāṇa*, of the *Saddharma-puṇḍarīka*, or of the *Aśokāvadāna* are adapted to form the basis of chronicles of the doings of the Sāṁkhya sage, the Śākya reformer or the Maurya monarch. In his *Early History of India* V. A. Smith complains that most writers upon Aśoka's reign have begun at the wrong end with the late legends, instead of at the right end with the contemporary inscriptions. Similarly most writers upon the life of Kṛishṇa have begun at the wrong end with the late epic and *Purāṇic* legends instead of at the right end with the early *Brāhmaṇas* and *Upanishads*.

On the strength of the late legends several scholars have come to the conclusion that Kṛishṇa Vāsudeva was not a human being, but a popular deity whose cult being foisted upon a dummy

1 iii, 17, 4.

2 xvi, 1-2.

Vishṇu gave rise to sectarian Vaishṇavism. For example, Barth says in his *Religions of India*[1] that Kṛishṇa is "beyond all doubt, a popular divinity" and that "there is a connection between the attainment of supremacy by Vishṇu and his identification with Kṛishṇa." "The supremacy of the Brāhmaṇic god was the result of his fusion with the popular god."

Barth considers Kṛishṇa to be a solar deity. "Like those of many solar deities his first appearances were beset with perils and obstructions of every kind. On the very night of his birth his parents had to remove him to a distance beyond the reach of his uncle king Kaṁsa who sought his life. In the Veda the sun in the form of Mārtāṇḍa is the eighth son born of Aditi, and his mother casts him off just as Devakī who is at times represented as an incarnation of Aditi removes Kṛishṇa. Conveyed to the opposite shore of the Yamunā and put under the care of the shepherd Nanda and his wife Yaçodā he was brought up as their son in the woods of Brindāban with his brother Balarāma. Arrived at adolescence the two brothers put to death Kaṁsa, and Kṛishṇa became king of the Yādavas. He took a determined side in the great struggle of the sons of Pāṇḍu against those of Dhṛitarāshṭra which forms the subject of the *Mahābhārata*. In the interval he had transferred the seat of his

[1] P. 166.

dominions to the fabulous city of Dwārakā, the city of gates, the gates of the West. It was here that he was overtaken himself and his race by the final catastrophe."

According to Hopkins[1] "The Vishṇu worship which grew about Kṛishṇa was probably at first an attempt to foist upon Vedic believers a sectarian god, by identifying the latter with a Vedic divinity." "The epic describes the overthrow of an old Brāhmaṇic Aryan race at the hands of the Pāṇḍavas, an unknown folk, whose King's polyandrous marriage is an historical trait, connecting the tribe closely with the polyandrous wild tribes located north of the Ganges. This tribe attacked the stronghold of Brāhmaṇism in the holy land about the present Delhi; and their patron god is the Gangetic Kṛishṇa."[2] "The simple original view of Kṛishṇa is that he is a god, the son of Devakī."[3]

Other scholars find in Kṛishṇa "a development from one of those vegetation deities that seem to have been so widely worshipped and to have obtained so strong a hold of men's devotion in all countries of the world. Such were the Semitic Adonis, the Egyptian Osiris and the Greek Dionysos. They mention his connection with cattle as Govinda, the vegetation spirit being usually

1 The Religions of India, p. 388.
2 R. I., pp. 466-67.
3 R. I., p. 467.

supposed to incarnate itself in such animals, his near relationship with Balarāma, who is supposed to be a god of harvest, his name Dāmodara, *i.e.*, the god 'with a cord round his belly,' a description which is supposed to be derived from wheat-sheaf, and most significant of all, the evidence of the *Mahābhāshya* of Patañjali that he appeared in a 'vegetation masque' contending with Kaṁsa for the possession of the Sun."[1] Dr. Keith, an ardent advocate of this theory, remarks,[2] "It is clear that from this original divine character of Kṛishṇa as the spirit of the reviving vegetation we can derive his whole character both as a child and as a hero, for the vegetation spirit has both sides in the Greek Dionysos who is in this aspect parallel to Kṛishṇa, and the legend of Kaṁsa is a mythological invention based on the ritual of (*a*) the childgod, and (*b*) the slaying of a rival—the old spirit of vegetation or some similar conception by the new spirit."

We shall not canvass in detail the views of Barth. His theory is of a piece with the brilliant study of Senart, in which the figure of Buddha is similarly resolved into a solar type and the history of the reformer becomes a sun-myth. Dr. Keith observes,[3] "It hardly seems possible to ascribe to Kṛishṇa an original solar character. His name

1 See Macnicol, *Indian Theism*, pp. 37-38.

2 J. R. A. S., 1915, p. 841.

3 J. R. A. S., 1908, p. 171.

tells seriously against it: the 'dark sun' requires more explanation than it seems likely to receive."

The theory of Hopkins rests on a mass of unproved hypothesis. There is no good reason to believe that the Pāṇḍavas were an "unknown folk connected with the wild tribes located north of the Ganges" and that Kṛishṇa was the "patron God" of the tribe. Hindu tradition is unanimous in representing the Pāṇḍavas as an offshoot of the Kuru race. In the *Mahābhārata* the epithet *Kurukulodvaha* is applied to Pāṇḍu[1] and to Yudhishṭhira.[2] The *Kaurava* affinity of the Pāṇḍus is known throughout the epic and is by no means confined only to the genealogical lists. Patañjali[3] too calls Bhīma, Nakula and Sahadeva Kurus.[4] The very name of the great Epic betrays the Bhārata (Kuru) connection of its principal heroes and combatants. The testimony of Buddhist literature points to the same conclusion. In the *Dasa-Brāhmaṇa Jātaka*[5] a king "of the stock of Yuddhiṭṭhila" reigning "in the kingdom of Kuru and the city called Indapatta" is distinctly called "Koravya," *i.e.*, Kauravya—"belonging to the Kuru race." In the *Kurudhamma Jātaka*[6] Dhanañjaya, king of Indapatta city, is called "the Kuru King." "He grew in Kuru righteousness, keeping the ten royal duties."

[1] i, 126, 33. [2] ii, 46, 5; iii, 17, 9.
[3] IV, I, 4. [4] Ind. Ant., I, 350.
[5] Cowell's Jātaka, Vol. IV, p. 227.
[6] Cowell's Jātaka, Vol. II, p. 251.

The polyandrous marriage of the Pāṇḍu king, which Hopkins considers to be an "historical trait," is no proof of the connection of the Pāṇḍavas with any non-Brāhmaṇic wild tribe. The marriage was approved by the Pañchālas, an undoubtedly Brāhmaṇic tribe. We learn also from the *Mahābhārata* that such marriages were prevalent among certain Brāhmaṇic Ṛishi families :—

"*Śruyate hi purāṇe' pi Jaṭilā nāma Gautamī*
Ṛishinadhyāsitavatī saptadharmabhṛitāmvarā
Tathaiva munijā Vārkshī tapobhirbhāvitātmanaḥ
Saṅgatābhūt daśa bhrātṛinekanāmnaḥ Pra-chetasaḥ" [1]

"I have heard in the *Purāṇa* that a lady named Jaṭilā, the foremost of all virtuous women belonging to the race of Gotama, had married seven *Ṛishis*. So also an ascetic's daughter named Vārkshī had in former times united herself in marriage with ten brothers bearing the same name of Prachetā and who were all of souls exalted by asceticism." The polyandrous marriage of the Prachetā brothers is clearly alluded to in the *Matsya* and *Brahma Purāṇas*.

The system of *Niyoga* prevalent among the Kurus of the *Madhyadeśa* was not far removed from fraternal polyandry, while the law (*Dharma*)

1 Mbh., i, 196, 14-16. *Cf. Matsya Purāṇa*, iv, 47-49, *Brahma Purāṇa*, ii, 46.

of marriage honoured by the Northern Kurus was admittedly lax.[1] Attention may, in this connection, be invited to the social environment disclosed by the stories of Mamatā[2] and Mādhavī.[3]

The name of the greatest of the Pāṇḍavas, Arjuna, is a thoroughly Brāhmaṇic name. It occurs in the *Mādhyandina* recension of the *Saṁhitā* of the *White Yajus* :—

" To obtain intrepidity, to obtain food, (I, the offerer, ascend) thee (O chariot) I, the inviolate Arjuna." [4]

A recent writer lays stress not only on the polyandrous marriage of the Pāṇḍus but on the drinking of blood by Bhīma[5] which, according to him, points to the Scythian affinity of the family. But a family custom can hardly be inferred from a solitary act of a single individual done in the heat of war expressly to fulfil a vow. As to the polyandrous marriage of Draupadî it is significant that in spite of the alleged family custom no other wife was shared by the brothers, and their children had no common wife. Śakas are often mentioned in the epic, particularly in the battle-books, but they are never represented as next of kin to the Pāṇḍus.

1 Mbh., 1, 122, 7.
2 Mbb., 1, 104, 9-10.
3 Mbh., V, 115 ff.
4 X, 21 ; Weber, *Ind. Lit.*, 115.
5 *Modern Review*, December, 1934.

There is no proof that any section of the Kuru people had a patron god named Kṛishṇa. Kṛishṇa is represented as a prince of the Vṛishṇi clan in the *Gītā* "which is unquestionably one of the older poems of the epic."[1] He is never called the patron god of any invading barbarous tribe.

The theory of those who assert that Kṛishṇa was a vegetation deity rests upon no better foundation. Kṛishṇa's connection with cattle is no proof that he was a vegetation deity. The connection of Moses with "the flock of Jethrow his father-in-law" is well known to students of the Bible.[2] The Yamunā region, the scene of Kṛishṇa's childhood, was renowned for its cattle even in the early Vedic period.[3] "May thes even times seven all-potent Maruts, (aggregated as) a single troop bestow upon me hundreds (of cattle): may I possess wealth of cows, renowned upon the (banks of) the Yamùnā—*Yamunāyāmadhi śrutamad rādho gavyam.*"[4] A Gobala Vārshṇa is mentioned as a teacher in the *Taittīriya Saṁhitā*[5] and the *Jaiminīya Upanishad Brāhmaṇa.*[6] Kṛishṇa's connection with cattle may, therefore, be an historical trait. There is yet another possibility. Kṛishṇa's names Govinda, Gopāla, Gopendra,

1 Hopkins, The Great Epic of India, p. 205.

2 Exodus, 3, 1.

3 Ṛig Veda, v, 52, 17.

4 *Cf.* Wilson, *Ṛig Veda*, iii, 328n.

5 III, 11, 9, 3.

6 I, 6, 1.

etc., may really be connected with the epithet *Gopā* applied in the Ṛig Veda to Vishṇu, the Brāhmaṇic god with whom Kṛishṇa came to be identified :—

" *Trīṇipadā vichakrame Vishṇurgopāadābhyaḥ* " [1]

Gopā may mean "protector of cows," [2] or "herdsman." [3] According to the *Ṛig Veda* [4] the highest step of Vishṇu is the dwelling of the "many horned swiftly moving cows." In the *Bodhāyana Dharma Sūtra* [5] Vishṇu is called Govinda and Dāmodara, but not yet Kṛishṇa or Vāsudeva. This probably suggests that the pastoral association of Vishṇu was independent of his identification with Kṛishṇa, and Govinda was *originally* an epithet of Vishṇu and possibly not of Kṛishṇa. Attention may in this connection be invited to the significant name "Vishṇu-gopa" occurring in the Allahabad Pillar Inscription of Samudra Gupta, belonging to the fourth century A.D.

We know that several Vedic epithets of Vishṇu were in the epics and the *Purāṇas* transferred to Kṛishṇa Vāsudeva. We have already seen that

1 R. V., i, 22, 18.

2 *Cf.* Ṛig Veda, x, 19, 4 : Macdonell and Keith, Vedic Index, Vol. I, p. 238.

3 Hopkins, The Religions of India, p. 57.

4 I, 154, 6.

5 II, 5, 24.

in the Ṛigveda Vishṇu is revered under the title "*Śipivishṭa.*"[1] Now this epithet is given to Kṛishṇa in the Great Epic.[2] In the *Śatapatha Brāhmaṇa*, i, 2,5,5, Vishṇu is called Vāmana ; in the *Mahābhārata*[3] Kṛishṇa receives the same epithet.

As regards Dāmodara we need only point out that it, too, occurs as an epithet of Vishṇu in the *Bodhāyana Dharma Sūtra*, before the identification of the deity with Kṛishṇa was thought of. The word does not necessarily mean "the God with a cord round his belly." It is used in an altogether different sense in the epic :—

> "*Devānām svaprakāśatvād*
> *damādDāmodaro vibhuḥ*"[4]

"That supreme soul is called Dāmodara because unlike the gods his effulgence is increate and his own, and also because he hath self-control (*Dama*) and great splendour."

We shall now consider the evidence of Patañjali. The passage on which Dr. Keith and others rely as supporting their theory runs as follows :—"*Vyamisrā dṛiśyante. Kechit Kaṁsa-bhaktā bhavanti kechid Vāsudeva bhaktāḥ. Varṇā-*

1 VII, 100, 5, 6.
2 XI, 43, 8; xii, 342, 72-73.
3 XII, 43, 12.
4 Mbh., v, 70, 8.

nyatvam khalvapi pushyanti. Kechit kālamukhā bhavanti kechidraktamukāḥ."

The slaying of Kaṁsa by Kṛishṇa was the subject of dramatic and pictorial representations in the time of Patañjali and the story was also narrated by word of mouth. According to Dr. Keith's interpretation of the *Mahābhāshya* passage quoted above, the *granthikas* or narrators while relating the fortunes of their subjects divided themselves into two parts ; those representing the followers of Kaṁsa had their faces blackened, *kālamukhāḥ*, those of Kṛishṇa had their faces red, *raktamukhāḥ*, and they expressed the feelings of both sides throughout the struggle from Kṛishṇa's birth to the death of Kaṁsa. "The mention of the colour of the two parties," says Keith, "is most significant ; red man slays black man ; the spirit of spring and summer prevails over the spirit of the dark winter. The parallel is too striking to be mistaken. We are entitled to say that in India, as in Greece, this primitve dramatic ritual slaying of winter is the source whence the drama is derived."[1]

But Keith's interpretation of the *Mahābhāshya* passage is by no means accepted by all. The meaning of the passage with its context is thus given by Bhandarkar :[2]

"The narrators give expression to what they know about them (Kaṁsa and Kṛishṇa) from

[1] J. R. A. S., 1911, p. 1008. [2] Ind. Ant., 1874, p. 16.

their birth to their death, and thus externally manifest what at the time exists internally, and that the things do exist internally or in the mind is shown in this way. They (the narrators) are of various kinds, some are adherents or devotees of Kaṁsa and some of Vāsudeva. Their countenances assume different colours; the faces of some (whose favourite hero is defeated) become dark, the faces of others red." Mr. R. P. Chanda points out[1] that according to several Indian interpreters of Patañjali it was not the *granthikas* or narrators who divided themselves into the parties, but the audience, some of whom sided with Kaṁsa and some others with Kṛishṇa, "the partisans of the former becoming pale with grief and the partisans of the latter becoming red with joy on the triumph of their hero." There is no reason to believe with Keith[2] that the Hindu audience consisted only of pious adorers of Kṛishṇa and therefore could not have included any who favoured Kaṁsa. The great epic testifies to the existence of men who were hostile to Kṛishṇa and spoke in terms of sympathy about Kaṁsa.[3] The pity excited in a section of the audience by the fate of Kaṁsa is probably reflected in the following passage of the *Vishṇu Purāṇa*:[4]

[1] *The Indo-Aryan Races*, pp. 94-95.
[2] *The Sanskrit Drama*, p. 35.
[3] Mbh., II, 41, 11, IX, 61, 27.
[4] V, 20, 78.

Tato hāhā kṛitaṁ sarvamāsīt tadraṅgamaṇḍalam
avajñayā hataṁ dṛishtvā Kṛishṇena Mathureśvaram.

The treatment accorded by Kṛishṇa to his maternal uncle earned for him the epithet *asādhu* in a fragment of a verse quoted by Patañjali (*asādhurmātule Kṛishṇa*) which must have been composed by some unknown *Kaṁsa-bhakta.* The hand of the *Kaṁsa-bhakta*, and people of that type, no less than that of the *Vāsudeva-bhakta*, is clearly visible in the composition of several passages of the Great Epic. In view of what has been noted above it is hardly permissible to surmise that we have in the *Mahābhāshya* an allusion to the slaying of the black man by the red man or to the slaying of winter by the spirit of spring and summer.

The pre-epical literature of the Hindus bears unequivocal testimony to the human character of Kṛishṇa. The *Chhāndogya Upanishad* which is one of the oldest Upanishads[1] and which undoubtedly belongs to the pre-Buddhistic period[2] mentions Kṛishṇa Devakīputra as a human sage, a disciple of the Ṛishi Ghora Āṅgirasa :

[1] Hopkins, *The Great Epic of India*, p. 385.

[2] Macdonell's *Hist. Sans. Lit.*, p. 226; Dr. R. L. Mitra's Introduction to Chh. Up., pp. 23-24.

[3] III, 17, 6.

"*Taddhaitad Ghora Āṅgirasaḥ Kṛishṇāya Devakīputrāyoktvovāchā pipāsa eva sa babhūva so'nta velāyāmetat trayam pratipadyeta—akshitamachyutamasi prāṇasanśitamasīti.*"

The human character of Kṛishṇa is also manifest in the Buddhist *Ghata Jātaka* as well as in the Jaina *Uttarādhyayana sūtra.*[1]

Max Müller denies[2] and Macdonell and Keith doubt the identity of Kṛishṇa Devakīputra of the epic and the *Purāṇas* with Kṛishṇa Devakīputra of the *Upanishad.* Referring to the Kṛishṇa of the *Upanishad* the latter scholars observe in the *Vedic Index,* "Tradition and several modern writers like Grierson, Garbe and Von Schroeder recognise in him the hero Kṛishṇa who later is deified. In their view he is a Kshatriya teacher of morals, as opposed to Brāhmaṇism. This is extremely doubtful. It appears better either to regard the coincidence of name as accidental, or to suppose that the reference is a piece of euhemerism."

Barth accepts the identity of the two Kṛishṇas but characterises the mention of Kṛishṇa in the *Upanishad* as an absolutely euhemerist representation.[3]

Dr. Keith has dealt fully with the subject in *J. R. A. S.,* 1915, pp. 548-550. "In the

1 Lecture XXII.

2 S. B. E. I., 52, n. 1.

3 R. I., p. 168,

Chhāndogya Upanishad we hear of a pupil Kṛṣṇa Devakīputra, of Ghora Āṅgirasa who is credited with certain doctrines. We are asked to believe that this is an historical reference to the Kṛṣṇa of the epic. It is a much more credible hypothesis on the theory of the identity of the Kṛṣṇas that we have in this Kṛṣṇa a euhemerism, a reduction to human rank of a tribal God and it is the only hypothesis which does not raise serious difficulties as to the date of the divinity of Kṛṣṇa and his appearance in the epic. That text never treats Kṛṣṇa as a mere ordinary mortal teacher ; when he teaches he reveals himself as the Supreme Being and we cannot ignore the fact that his divine nature is clearly known throughout the epic, which in a part claimed as old by Garbe (II, 2291) calls him *Gopījanavallabha* revealing him already as the beloved of the Gopīs, a feature which sits oddly on a presumed warrior-teacher, but which accords well with a god of Kṛṣṇa's type closely connected with pastoral life. Moreover, it is impossible to ignore the fact that in the epic Kṛṣṇa appears in his actions and his practical advice in a very different aspect from the Kṛṣṇa of the Upaniṣad, who appears in a passage where among other virtues the telling of truth is inculcated."[1]

In his *Early History of the Dekkan,*[2] Sir R. G. Bhandarkar points out that though a *Mahā-*

[1] Chh., iii, 17, 4. [2] P. 8 (old edition).

bhārata existed before Pāṇini and Āśvalāyana, it is highly questionable whether our present text is the same as that which existed in their times. On the contrary, the probability is that the work has been added to from time to time; and the text itself has undergone such corruption that no one can be positively certain that a particular word was not foisted into it in comparatively modern times. Hopkins shows in his *Great Epic of India* that the "Pāṇḍu epic as we have it represents a period subsequent not only to Buddhism 500 B.C. but to the Greek invasion 300 B.C."[1] Now, we know from the Besnagar Inscription that Vāsudeva who, judging from the context, was to Pāṇini only a Kshatriya worthy,[2] was in the second century B.C. recognised as "the God of gods." Is it, therefore, strange that the present *Mahābhārata* treats Kṛishṇa as a divine teacher? It is perfectly intelligible that a work representing a period subsequent to 300 B.C.—a time when the apotheosis of Vāsudeva was an established fact—should reveal him as a god. It is equally obvious that such a work cannot be accepted as an authority for characterising as a piece of euhemerism the mention of Kṛishṇa as a human pupil in a book which was composed before the rise of Buddhism in the sixth century B.C. In the

[1] G. E., I, p. 391.

[2] See Weber's Ind. Lit., p. 185, n.

Saddharmapuṇḍarīka [1] Buddha is not merely *deva*; he is *devātideva*. Will any one contend on the strength of this statement that the mention of Buddha as a human teacher in the *Dhammachakkappavattanasutta* is a piece of euhemerism?

We have already expressed our views regarding the pastoral associations of Kṛishṇa. There is no inherent improbability in Kṛishṇa's being a shepherd as well as a warrior-teacher. Moses and Mahomed furnish good parallels. It is, however, possible that the tales about the pastoral Kṛishṇa really arose from the Vedic legend of Vishṇu Gopā, just as the story of the Vāmana incarnation arose out of the legend of Vishṇu Urukrama.

With reference to Keith's remarks regarding the difference between the characters of the Epic and Upanishadic Kṛishṇas, it may be said that in the *Aśokāvadāna*, the Ceylonese Chronicles and the *Si-yu-ki* Aśoka appears in his actions and his practical advice in a very different aspect from the Aśoka of the Fifth and Thirteenth Rock Edicts. Are we to conclude from this that the Aśoka of the inscriptions is not identical with the Aśoka of the Chronicles? Again, Keith ignores the fact that the telling of truth is inculcated by the Epic Kṛishṇa in the *Gītā*, xvi, 2, and in several other passages of the *Mahābhārata*, *e.g.*,

1 vii, 31; *cf.* Trenckner, *Milinda pañho*, p. 401—*Bhagavatā devādidevena*.

"*Brahma satyaṁdamaḥ śaucham*
dharmo hrîḥ śrīrdhṛiti kshamā
yatra tatra rame nityam
ahaṁ satyena te śape" [1]

"Where there are sacred knowledge, *truth*, self-control, purity, righteousness, modesty, moral splendour, fortitude and forbearance, there I am also to be found."

Dr. Keith next goes on to say, "It is, however, of course possible that the similarity of name is a mere accident: metronymics are very frequent in the *Vaṁśas* of the Upaniṣads, and Kṛṣṇa is not rarely found as a non-divine name ; the only point of doubt in this view is the rarity of Devakī, but this is not conclusive ; Professor Garbe himself resigns his former view that the Patañjalis of the Mahābhāṣya and of the Yoga are identical. Nor can a third possibility be excluded: Kṛṣṇa as a god and a teacher may differ, but Devakīputra may be borrowed by the former from the latter, though this is less probable. We must, to be candid, recognize that our evidence is insufficient to decide the precise facts, and that we cannot build on it the edifice of the Kṛṣṇa who founded the Bhāgavata sect as a mere man. The epic has a god, the Upaniṣad a man, and the means of connexion are not apparent."

[1] Mbh., VII, 179, 29.

It is not so easy to refute an improbable historical theory as it is to propound it, but on the other hand the *onus probandi* rests upon him that propounds it. Dr. Keith admits that his evidence "is insufficient to decide the precise facts," but nevertheless remarks that the similarity between the names of the two Kṛishṇas may be a mere accident as in the case of the Patañjalis of the *Mahābhāshya* and of the *Yoga*. We readily admit that a mere similarity of names is no proof of identity. But in the case of the two Kṛishṇas the similarity extends further than this. The epic Kṛishṇa is the son of Devakī,[1] the Kṛishṇa of the *Upanishad* is also called the son of Devakī. The epic Kṛishṇa is often styled *Achyuta*. The epithet, as Hill points out, figures in the *Upanishad* passage about the pupil of Ghora. The teacher of the Upanishadic Kṛishṇa belonged to a family (Āṅgirasa) closely associated with the Bhojas,[2] the kindreds of the Epic Kṛishṇa.[3] The Kṛishṇa of the *Upanishad* and his preceptor Ghora Āṅgirasa were worshippers of the sun. We are told in the *Śānti-parva* of the *Mahābhārata* [4] that the *Sātvata-vidhi* expounded by the epic Kṛishṇa had been declared in days of yore by the sun himself, *Prāk-śūrya-mukha-niḥśrita,* and in the *Karṇa-parva*

1 Mbh., i, 190, 33; iii, 29, 46; etc.

2 *Ṛig Veda*, iii, 53, 7.

3 Mbh., ii, 14, 32-34,

4 335, 19.

Āṅgirasī śruti is praised by Kṛishṇa as the best of all revealed texts, *śrutināmuttamā śrutiḥ.*[1] The pupil of Ghora is taught the worship of the "noblest of all lights," *Jyotiruttamamiti*, " high above all darkness," *tamasaspari*, and also the virtues of *Tapodānamārjjavam ahimsā satya-vachanam.* The Epic Kṛishṇa teaches practically the same thing in the *Gītā* [2]—

" *Jyotishāmapi tajjyotis tamasaḥ param uchyate.*"

" *Dānam damaścha yajñaścha svādhyāyam tapa*
ārjjavam ahimsā satayam...."

Furthermore, the Great Epic has preserved distinct traces of the original character of Kṛishṇa as a human being. Kṛishṇa says in the *Udyoga-parva* :—

Ahaṁhi tat karishyāmi
paraṁ purushakārataḥ
daivantu na mayā śakyaṁ
karmakarttuṁ kathañchana.[3]

"I will do all that can be done by human exertion at its best. But I shall, by no means, be able to control what is providential."

The statement that Devakīputra may be borrowed by the epic from the *Upanishad* requires no comment ; we have already seen that there are

[1] 69, 85.
[2] xiii, 18 ; xvi, 1-2.
[3] Mbh., v, 79, 5-6.

other "means of connexion" besides the metronymic which go far to prove the identity of the two Kṛishṇas.

We have seen that the arguments of scholars who hold that Kṛishṇa Devakīputra was originally a deity do not bear scrutiny. We have also seen that there can be no reasonable objection to his identity with Kṛishṇa Devakīputra mentioned in one of the oldest *Upanishads*. The pre-epical literature of the Hindus knows a human Kṛishṇa but is silent about a deity Kṛishṇa. Buddhist and Jaina traditions clearly refer to Vāsudeva as a human hero. Even the *Mahābhārata* preserves traces of the original human character of Kṛishṇa. The conclusion, therefore, is irresistible that he was a real man. The divine nature of Kṛishṇa known throughout the greater part of the epic belonging in its present form to a period subsequent to the rule of the Scythians, Greeks, and Bactrians [1] would certainly not appear strange to those who will notice the appearance of Buddha among a crowd of heterogeneous deities in the monuments of the Indo-Scythian period.[2] In the case of Kapila we find another instance of a human teacher being raised to the dignity of a divine being in the epic.[3]

1 Mbh., iii, 188, 35.

2 V. Smith, E. H. I., 3rd Edition, p. 266.

3 *Cf.* Mbh., iii, 47, 18 ; vii, 220, 21 ; Hopkins, *The Great Epic of India*, p. 98.

We have tried to prove that Kṛishṇa Vāsudeva was a man. There remains the further question, "was he a hero who rose step by step to the rank of divinity, or was he a monotheistic reformer, a theistic Buddha before Buddha's day, who later like the Buddha himself was deified by his disciples ?" Dr. Macnicol suggests "it is possible that he was a famous prince of the Sātvata race and on his death was deified." We admit that there is much to be said for this view. Kṛishṇa appears as a disciple of a *Ṛishi* in the *Chhāndogya Upanishad*, but that does not show that he was himself a teacher. The *Ghata Jātaka* knows him only as a prince and a warrior, not as a leader of thought. The teaching contained in the *Gītā* is attributed to him, but that poem by its reference to the *Brahmasūtras* [1] presupposes the existence of the classical Upanishads, while Kṛishṇa himself is mentioned in one of the oldest Upanishads. The other works attributed to Kṛishṇa, *e.g.*, the *Anugītā* and the *Brāhmaṇagītā* are even later than the *Bhagavadgītā*.

On the other hand, it may be said that the *Chhāndogya Upanishad* does not pretend to give a life history of Kṛishṇa. Its reference to him is incidental ; and though it does not represent him as a teacher, it yet shows that he came into contact with a leader of thought, and learnt several

[1] Gītā, xiii, 5.

doctrines. The *Jātaka* knows Vāsudeva Kaṇha only as a prince and a warrior, but what more can we expect from a Buddhist work of this kind ? Lastly, the ascription of the entire *Gītā* to Kṛishṇa may well be looked upon with suspicion, but the fact remains that when the Pāṇḍu epic was being written Kṛishṇa was remembered not only as a hero, but as a teacher. If Kṛishṇa was only a hero, if the fundamental doctrines of the *Bhāgavatas* were not taught by him, but by some unknown person, we are driven to the assumption that the ancient *Bhāgavatas* forgot or suppressed the name of the Master "from whom has flowed through the centuries until to-day the stream of Bhakti in India." In this connection it may be pointed out that though the *Gītā* as a whole is posterior to the classical Upanishads, its fundamental doctrines may really have been taught by Kṛishṇa Devakīputra. For it will be shown in the next lecture that some of these doctrines agree almost *verbatim* with those which Kṛishṇa learnt from his Guru Ghora Âṅgirasa.

The fact that Kṛishṇa was a human teacher is admitted by eminent scholars like Sir R. G. Bhandarkar, Dr. Seal, Bühler, Grierson and Garbe.[1]

1 The *Indian Antiquary*, 1889, p. 189 ; *Comparative Studies in Vaishṇavism and Christianity*, p. 10 ; *Ind. Ant.*, 1894, p. 248 ; *Ind. Ant.*, 1908, p. 253 ; Garbe, *Philosophy of Ancient India*, pp. 83-85.

LECTURE II

THE LIFE OF KṚISHṆA VĀSUDEVA AND THE EARLY PROGRESS OF BHĀGAVATISM.

If Kṛishṇa is a human teacher, the question naturally arises when he lived. If the traditional connection of Kṛishṇa with the battle of Kurukshetra has any foundation in fact, then it must be admitted that he lived before the compilation of the *Kāṭhaka Saṁhitā* of the *Yajurveda*, for, one of his traditional contemporaries, Dhṛitarāshṭra Vaichitravīrya, a prominent figure in the Kurukshetra story, is mentioned in the *Kāṭhaka*.[1]

In the Aihole inscription of the Chalukya king Pulakeśin II, dated *Śaka* 556 (expired), *i.e.*, A.D. 634-35, it is stated that at that time 3,735 years had passed since the Bhārata war, *i.e.*, the battle of Kurukshetra. The date of the battle according to this calculation is 3102 B.C., which is the starting point of the so-called *Kali-Yuga* era. But, as pointed out by Fleet,[2] the reckoning was not founded in Vedic times. It is an invented one, devised by the Hindu astronomers and chronologists for the purposes of their calculations some thirty-five centuries after the initial point which they assigned to it. As a matter of fact another school

[1] Weber, Ind. Lit., p. 90 n.

[2] *JRAS*, 1911, pp. 479 ff., 675 ff.

of Hindu astronomers and historians represented by Vṛiddhagarga, Varāhamihira and Kalhaṇa placed the heroes of the Kurukshetra story 653 years after the beginning of the *Kali Yuga* and 2,526 years before the Śaka era (*i.e.*, in B.C. 2449).[1] A recent writer tries to reconcile the conflicting views presented by the two schools of chronologists by suggesting that the *Śaka-kāla* of Varāha is really *Śākya-kāla*, *i.e.*, the era of the Buddha's *Nirvāna*. This view is not only opposed to the evidence of Kalhaṇa but is flatly contradicted by Bhaṭṭotpala who explains *Śaka-kāla* of the *Bṛihat-Saṁhitā* passage as *Śakanṛipa-kāla* (era of the Śaka *king*).[2]

A third tradition is recorded by the compilers of the *Purāṇas*. A verse found with slight variants in the *Matsya*, *Vāyu*, *Brahmāṇḍa*, *Vishṇu*, and *Bhāgavata Purāṇas* states that "from Mahāpadma Nanda's inauguration to Parikshit's birth the interval is known as 1,015 years." (1,050 or 1,500 according to some manuscripts) :—

Yāvat Parikshito janma
yāvan Nandābhishechanam
evaṁ varshasahasraṁtu
jñeyampañchadaśottaram.[3]

[1] *Bṛihat Saṁhitā*, xiii, 3; *Rājataraṅginī*, i, 48-56.

[2] The *Bṛihat-Saṁhitā* by Varāha with the commentary of Bhaṭṭotpala, edited by Sudhākara Dvivedī, p. 281—Vizianagram Sanskrit Series, Vol. X, Pt. I, 1895.

[3] Pargiter, *Dynasties of the Kali Age*, p. 58.

The date of Nanda's accession according to Geiger is 343 B.C.[1]

343 B.C. + 1015 = 1358 B.C.
343 B.C. + 1050 = 1393 B.C.
343 B.C. + 1500 = 1843 B.C.

c. 1400 B.C. (or *c.* 1800 B.C.) in round numbers is, therefore, the Purāṇic date of Parkshit's birth which, according to the *Mahābhārata*, immediately followed the battle of Kurukshetra.

In view of the conflicting tradition regarding the date of the battle, we cannot say that implicit reliance can be placed on the *early* chronology of the astronomers or of the poets and chroniclers who compiled the epic, the Purāṇas and the annals of Kashmir.

Kṛishṇa certainly lived before the Buddha, as he is mentioned in the *Chhāndogya Upanishad* which is a pre-Buddhistic work. The evidence of the *Ghata Jātaka*, where Kṛishṇa is mentioned as a brother and contemporary of Ghata, the *Bodhisattva*, points to the same conclusion. His *Guru* Ghora Āṅgirasa is also mentioned in the *Kaushītaki Brāhmaṇa*,[2] and the *Kâṭhaka Saṁhitā* [3] which are also pre-Buddhistic works. Jaina tradition makes Kṛishṇa a contemporary of Arishṭanemi or Neminātha, the 22nd Tīrthankara who is

[1] Mahāvaṁsa, p. xlvi.
[2] xxx, 6.
[3] i, 1.

the immediate predecessor of Pārśvanātha, the 23rd Tīrthankara.[1] As Pārśvanātha probably flourished about 817 B.C.,[2] Kṛishṇa, if Jaina tradition is to be believed, must have lived long before the closing years of the ninth century B.C. The name of the Vṛishṇi or Sātvata family to which Kṛishṇa belonged is unknown to the Ṛig Veda but is frequently referred to in the *Brāhmaṇas*. The overthrow of the family is alluded to by Kauṭilya in the *Arthaśāstra* attributed to him.

Regarding the life history of Kṛishṇa Vāsudeva we know very little if we leave aside the epic and *Purāṇic* legends. "As far as it is known," says an American writer in speaking of the great Athenian sage, "the life of Socrates, in its merely outward bodily incident, may be told in a paragraph." Such unfortunately is also the case with Vāsudeva.

For a life of Kṛishṇa our sources are :—

(1) The *Chhāndogya Upanishad*.

(2) The incidental notices in the *Indika* of Megasthenes, and the *Mahābhāshya* of Patañjali.

(3) The Buddhist *Ghata Jātaka* and the Jaina *Uttarādhyayana Sūtra*.

(4) The *Mahābhārata*, the *Harivaṁśa*, the *Purāṇas*, and the sectarian *Upanishads*.

[1] Jacobi, *Jaina Sūtras*, Part I, pp. 271-279; II, pp. 112-19.

[2] Mrs. Stevenson's *Heart of Jainism*, p. 48.

The exact date of the *Chhāndogya Upanishad* is not known, but it is certainly pre-Buddhistic. Referring to the date of the Upanishads, Macdonell says :[1] " The earliest of them can hardly be dated later than about 600 B.C. since some important doctrines first met with in them are presupposed by Buddhism. They may be divided chronologically on internal evidence into four classes. The oldest group consisting in chronological order of the *Bṛihadāraṇyaka*, *Chhāndogya*, *Taittirīya*, *Aitareya*, *Kaushītaki*, is written in prose which still suffers from the awkwardness of the *Brāhmaṇa* style." Dr. R. L. Mitra in the introduction to his translation of the *Chhāndogya Upanishad* observes,[2] " An attempt has lately been made to prove that some of the doctrines in the *Chhāndogya* in common with the other *Upanishads* are of Buddhist origin, and consequently the work itself is of a post-Buddhistic era. But the argument used to establish this hypothesis is founded on a *petitio principii*. It begins by assigning to Buddha what, as philosophic ideas, were probably well known long before they were adopted by the founder of Buddhism, and then argues the works in which they occur to be posterior to the system of Śākyasinha ; when the character of those very works indicates the assumption to be utterly unfounded. The Upanishads belong to an age of

[1] Hist. Sans. Lit., p. 226. [2] Pp. 23-24.

search and enquiry, the Sāṅkhya to doubt following enquiry, and the Bauddha philosophy to an epoch when doubt and disbelief taking possession of men's minds, dared at last to raise their heads boldly against God Himself. The hypothesis of the post-Buddhistic origin of the Upanishads would reverse this order, and begin with the infidelity of Śākya to be followed by the doubt of Kapila and then the enquiry of the Upanishads."

The accepted dates of the *Indika* of Megasthenes and of the *Mahābhāshya* of Patañjali are, as is well known, the fourth and second centuries B.C., respectively. As regards the date of the *Jātaka*, bas-reliefs of the second century B.C. have been found illustrating a number of *Jātaka* stories. The *Jātaka* Book, according to Rhys Davids,[1] is an example of that pre-Epic form of literature of which there are so many other shorter specimens preserved for us in the earlier canonical texts. The date of the *Uttarādhyayana* is also not certain. Jaina tradition attributes its lectures to Mahāvīra. Its *niryukti* or commentary is ascribed to Bhadrabāhu (fourth century B.C.) in the *Vṛitti* of the *Ṛishimaṇḍala Sūtra*.[2] It forms a part of the Jaina Canon which was reduced to writing in or about the fifth century A.D.

The date of the *Mahābhārata* has been discussed with great acumen by Washburn Hopkins who

[1] *Buddhist India*, p. 206.

[2] See Jacobi, *The Kalpa Sūtra of Bhadrabāhu*, 1879, p. 12.

has given much study to this treasure house of Indian religious lore. It is true that Pāṇini and Āśvalāyana knew a *Mahābhārata*, but their epic was not our present epic. "The Pāṇḍu epic as we have it represents a period subsequent not only to Buddhism 500 B.C., but to the Greek invasion 300 B.C. Buddhist supremacy already decadent is implied by the passages which allude contemptuously to the *eḍūkas* or Buddhistic monuments as having ousted the temples of the gods. Thus in iii, 190,65 'They will revere *eḍūkas*, they will neglect the gods;' *ib.* 67, 'the earth shall be piled with *eḍūkas*, not adorned with god-houses.' With such expressions may be compared the thoroughly Buddhistic epithet, *Cāturmahārājika*, in xii, 339, 40, and Buddhistic philosophy as expounded in the same book."

"The Greeks are described as a western people (north-western, with Kāmbojas), famous as fighters." "The Romans, Romakas, are mentioned but once, in a formal list of all possible peoples, ii, 51,17 (Cannibals, Chinese, Greeks, Persians, Scythians, and other barbarians), and stand thus in marked contrast to the Greeks and Persians, Pahlavas, who are mentioned very often. It is clear from this that, while the Greeks were familiar, the Romans were as yet but a name. Further, the distinct prophecy that 'Scythians, Greeks and Bactrians will rule unrighteously in the evil age to come,' which occurs in iii, 188, 35 is too clear a statement to be ignored or explained away. When this was written the peoples mentioned had already ruled Hindustan."

The *Śānti-parva* mentions Yāska, the author of the *Nirukta* [1] and Vārshagaṇya,[2] the Sāṁkhya philosopher who probably flourished in the fifth century after Christ.[3]

The *Harivaṁśa* is regarded as a part of the *Mahābhārata*. From the Khoh Copper Plate Inscription of Śarvanātha dating from 532-33 A.D. we learn that the *Mahābhārata* in the sixth century A.D. consisted of 1,00,000 *ślokas* (*Śatasāhasrī-Saṁhitā*). As it would have been impossible to speak even approximately of 1,00,000 verses without the *Harivaṁśa*, scholars think that the work must have formed a part of the *Mahābhārata* in the sixth century A.D. There is some reason to believe that the *Harivaṁśa*, or at least a part of it, existed before Aśvaghosha, for, an important episode about Bhīshma mentioned in the twentieth chapter of the work, but not in the *Mahābhārata*, is alluded to in the *Buddhacharita*, and two verses from the *Harivaṁśa* are quoted in the *Vajrasūchī*.[4] But the *Harivaṁśa* is later than the Greek invasion and

[1] 342, 73.

[2] 318, 59.

[3] *JRAS*, 1905, pp. 47-51.

[4] Raychaudhuri, *Studies in Indian Antiquities*, p. 174 ; Winternitz, *A History of Indian Literature*, Vol. I, p. 464.

the beginning of commercial intercourse with the Roman Empire for it mentions the Denarius.[1]

The genuine *Purāṇas* which relate the Kṛishṇa story cannot be placed earlier than the third or fourth century A.D. because they contain lists of kings of India down to the Andhra or Gupta monarchs. The original texts cannot perhaps be placed later than 500 A.D. because *all* the eighteen *Purāṇas* are mentioned in the last book of the *Māhābhārata* which attained its present bulk before the sixth century. Bas-reliefs have been found at Bādāmi illustrating a number of *Purāṇic* stories about Kṛishṇa, which date from the sixth century A.D.[2]

We have independent proof of the existence of the *Vāyu*, *Agni*, *Mārkaṇḍeya*, *Bhāgavata* and *Skanda Purāṇas* in some shape in the seventh century A.D.[3] Telang points out that the *Śaṅkara Vijaya* attributed to Ānandagiri, a pupil of Śaṅkara, contains quotations from the *Skanda*, *Mārkaṇḍeya*, *Bṛihannāradīya*, *Vishṇu* and *Bhāgavata* Purāṇas.[4] But the antiquity of the work is not above suspicion. Mr. K. G. Sesha Aiyar says that Abhinavagupta, a writer of the tenth century, refers to the *Bhāgavata Purāṇa* in his commentary on the *Gītā*.[5] It has been pointed

1 See *Vishṇu-parva*, 55, 50 and Hopkins, *G.E.I.*, p. 387.

2 *MASI*, No. 25, *Bas-reliefs of Badami* by R. D. Banerji, pp. 19, 24 ff.

3 V. Smith's E. H. I., *Age of the Purāṇas*.

4 *Indian Antiquary*, 1876, 290.

5 *IHQ*, 1931, 728.

out by Sir Ramkrishṇa Bhandarkar[1] that the *Mukundamālā*, attributed to the Ālvār Kulaśekhara, contains a verse from the same *Purāṇa*.[2] The sectarian *Upanishads* evidently belong to the Purāṇic age.

Whatever may be the date of Kṛishṇa, he certainly lived before 600 B.C. as he is mentioned in the *Chhāndogya Upanishad.* To reconstruct a life of the teacher on the evidence of the *Harivaṁśa* or the *Purāṇas* which in their present shape are separated by an interval of many centuries from his time, will be building castles on a morass. The same remark applies to the sectarian *Upanishads*.

The evidence of the *Mahābhārata* must be used with caution. Though certain parts of the poem are undoubtedly old and contain genuine historical tradition, yet the date of the work as a whole is not far removed from the age of the *Purāṇas* ; and it is not always easy to separate the kernel of the epic from the husk. We shall make use only of those portions of the epic account which are corroborated by external evidence.

The *Jātaka* and the Jaina *Sūtra*, too, cannot be implicitly relied on. They are in no sense historical records and contain a good deal of what is untrustworthy. But they have the merit of

[1] *Vaiṣṇavism, etc.*, pp. 49-50.

[2] xi, 2, 36.

preserving versions of the Kṛishṇa story free from the extravaganzas of the epic and the Purāṇas. The *Indika* and the *Mahābhāshya* contain important hints, but being post-Buddhistic their value is considerably less than that of the *Chhāndogya Upanishad* ; and it is from the last work that we can expect to get the most authentic information regarding the founder of the *Bhāgavata* religion.

The unanimity of Hindu, Jaina and Buddhist tradition would seem to indicate that Vāsudeva was really a scion of the royal family, Yādava, Vṛishṇi or Sātvata, of Mathurā, "Upper Madhurā" according to the *Ghata Jātaka*. The conclusion accords with the statement of Megasthenes regarding the connection of the Indian Herakles with the Sourasenoi and Methora.[1] The city of Mathurā is apparently referred to as the *Mahāsthāna*, "great place," of the Blessed Vāsudeva in an inscription of the time of the Śaka Satrap Śoḍāsa, assignable to the first century A.D. The name of his father is Vasudeva according to the epic, the *Uttarādhyayana Sūtra* and the Aphsaḍ Inscription of Ādityasena, Vasudeva Ānakadundubhi according to the *Purāṇas*[2] and Upasāgara according to the *Ghata Jātaka*. The name of his mother was certainly Devakī.[3] The existence of a brother

[1] McCrindle's *Megasthenes and Arrian*, p. 201.

[2] Matsya, 46, 2; Vāyu, 96, 144.

[3] Chh. Up., iii, 17, 6; Mbh., i, 109, 33; the *Uttarādhyayana*; the Bhitarī Pillar Inscription of Skanda Gupta.

named Baladeva or Saṅkarshaṇa is vouched for by all the authorities[1] including the *Mahābhāshya* which contains the passage—*Saṅkarshaṇa dvitīyasya balam Kṛishṇasya vardhatām.*

The story of Kṛishṇa's questionable relations with the Gopīs is found only in the *Harivaṁśa* and the *Purāṇas,* and is not met with in the *Jātaka* or the epic, not even in the reviling scene in the *Sabhā-parva.* Even a critic like Hopkins observes :[2] "Modern writers......forget that the lower side of Kṛishṇa is one especially Purāṇic. In short they read history backwards......In Kṛishṇa's case the tricky, vulgar, human side is a later aspect, which comes to light most prominently in the Genealogy of Vishṇu and in the Vishṇu Purāṇa, modern works which in this regard contrast strongly with the older epic,...It is not till he becomes a great, if not the greatest, god that tales about his youthful performances when he condescended to be born in low life begin to rise."

We have practically no authentic information as to the way in which the childhood of Kṛishṇa was spent. The most probable view is that he lived with his preceptor Ghora Āṅgirasa and returned to Mathurā on arriving at adolescence. The *Purāṇas* mention Sāndīpani as a teacher of

1 Mbh., ii, 79, 23; Cowell's *Jātaka,* Vol. IV, p. 51; the *Uttarādhyayana.*

2 *The Religions of India,* p. 467.

Kṛishṇa. But that sage is said to have given instruction in the science of arms and not in religion or philosophy, and the Yādava prince is reputed to have studied under him after the overthrow of Kaṁsa at Mathurā. The story of Sāndīpani may or may not be historical. But it does not in any way conflict with the theory of Kṛishṇa's residence with Ghora for purposes of religious and philosophical studies.

The idea of the pastoral Kṛishṇa and some of the Purāṇic stories about his childhood are evidently borrowed from the Vishṇu legends in the Vedic literature. In the *Ṛigveda*, 1,22,18, Vishṇu is called *Gopā*. In 1,154,6 we have a reference to the many-horned swiftly-moving cows in the abode of Vishṇu. In 1,155,6, Vishṇu is described as a youth who is no longer a child. In VII, 99,5, we have the story of Sambara's defeat at the hands of Vishṇu. In the *Bodhāyana-Dharma-sūtra* [1] Vishṇu is called Govinda and Dāmodara though there is no indication of his identification with Kṛishṇa Vāsudeva. But though the idea of a pastoral Kṛishṇa may have been borrowed from the Vedas its development was clearly due to some such tribe as the Ābhiras who were closely connected with the Pāṇḍu migration to the south.[2]

1 ii, 5, 24.

2 *Cf.* Kanakasabhai's *Tamils Eighteen Hundred Years Ago*, p. 57.

The story of Kṛishṇa's quarrel with Kaṁsa has some appearance of reality. It is related in the *Jātaka* as well as in the epic and is alluded to by Patañjali.

It is not a little surprising that the *Jātaka* is silent about the connection of Kṛishṇa with the Pāṇḍavas. The Pāṇḍavas are known to many *Jātakas*,[1] but nowhere is there any reference to their connection with Vāsudeva. But the story of Herakles and Pandaia narrated by Greek writers undoubtedly proves the antiquity of the tradition regarding Kṛishṇa's connection with the Pāṇḍu family. In the Great Epic Kṛishṇa figures as a friend and counsellor of the Pāṇḍavas, especially in their struggles against Jarāsandha, King of Magadha, and Duryodhana, King of the Kurus. As said by Smith, the modern critic fails to find sober history in the bardic tales about these feuds. But as deductions regarding Kṛishṇa's character have been freely made on the strength of these legends, they cannot "only be mentioned and laid aside." Hopkins observes in his *Religions of India*,[2] "the Kṛishṇa of the epic is a sly, unscrupulous fellow, continually suggesting and executing acts that are at variance with the knightly code of honour." That the remark is one-sided will be apparent to every reader of the Great Epic.

1 *E.g.*, the *Kunāla Jātaka*; the *Kurudhamma Jātaka*; the *Dhūmakāri Jātaka*; the *Dasa Brāhmaṇa Jātaka*.

2 P. 388.

Hopkins takes note only of the few episodes in the epic in which Kṛishṇa's character appears in an unfavourable light, but ignores the numerous episodes in which he appears as the embodiment of all that is good. He himself says that "the priests of Çiva were the last to retouch the poem"[1] and that "there is as much Çivaism in the poem as there is Vishṇuism."[2] Sectarian rancour may have been at the bottom of this darkening of the character of Vāsudeva.[3] Indications of sectarian animosity are not rare in the epic. In xii, 342, 109-116, there is a clear reference to a quarrel between Nārāyaṇa and Śiva.

That a section of the orthodox Brāhmaṇists were not favourably disposed towards Kṛishṇa and his worship is apparent from the reviling scene of the *Sabhā-parva* :—

Yadyayaṁ jagataḥ kartā
yathainaṁ mūrkha manyase
kasmānna Brāhmaṇaṁ samyag
ātmānamavagachchhati.[4]

1 R. I., p. 356 n.

2 *Op. cit.*, p. 349, n.

3 The tricky vulgar side of Kṛishṇa's character may have been partly derived from the Vishṇuite legends in the Vedic literature. In *Ṛig Veda*, i, 61, 7, Vishṇu stole the cooked mess. In i, 154 he receives the epithet *Kuchara*, 'who does a blamable action.' Vishṇu often resorts to cunning device to help Indra and other friends and to discomfit the Asuras (Keith *Religion and Philosophy of the Veda*, I, 110-11) just as Kṛishṇa does to assist Arjuna, son of Indra, and his brothers.

4 Mbh., ii, 42, 6.

"If this one (Kṛishṇa) is the lord of the universe as this fool representeth him, why doth he not regard himself as a Brāhmaṇa?"

Kṛishṇa is not the only teacher whose character has been blackened by hostile poets. In the *Rāmāyaṇa*,[1] the Buddha is branded as a thief and an atheist :—

> "*Yathā hi chauraḥ sa tathāhi Buddha*
> *Stathāgataṁ nāstikamatra viddhi.*
> *Tasmāddhi yaḥ śakyatamaḥ prajānāṁ*
> *Sa nāstike nābhimukho budhaḥ syāt.*"

Although recognised as an *avatāra* in the *Bhāgavata Purāṇa* he is said to have come down not to establish religion but to delude the enemies of the gods[2] :—

> "*Tataḥ kalau sampravṛitte saṁmohāya suradvishām*
> *Buddhonāmnā'ñjanasutaḥ Kīkaṭeshu bhavishyati.*"

In the *Life of Madhva* Śaṅkara is represented as an incarnation of a demon.[3]

In order to get the real history of the Sātvatas or Vṛishṇis and their prophet Kṛishṇa Devakîputra we must turn to the *Saṁhitās*, *Brāhmaṇas*

[1] ii, 109, 34. *Cf.* the *Kapālin's* utterance in the *Mattavilāsa-prahasana—Namaḥ Kharapaṭāyeti vaktavyaṁ yena choraśāstraṁ praṇītaṁ. Athavā Kharapaṭā-dapyasmin adhikāre Buddha evādhikaḥ.*

[2] Bh. Purāṇa, 1, 3, 24.

[3] C. N. Krishnaswami Aiyar, *Srī Saṅkarāchārya*, p. 5.

and the *Upanishads*. *Gobala* Vārshṇa is mentioned as a teacher in the *Taittirīya Saṁhitā*[1] and the *Jaiminīya Upanishad Brāhmaṇa*.[2] Vārshṇeya is the patronymic of Śūsha in the *Taittirīya Brāhmaṇa*.[3] Vārshṇya is the patronymic of a man in the *Śatapatha Brāhmaṇa*.[4] The Satvats are mentioned in the *Śatapatha*[5] and the *Aitareya Brāhmaṇas*.[6] The inference is legitimate that the Satvats, Sātvatas or Vṛishṇis were a famous people in the Brāhmaṇic age, and that they had produced at least one teacher of repute in the early Vedic times. The Aryan nationality of the Sātvatas is hinted at in the Tusam Rock inscription.

It was among this people that Kṛishṇa was born. We learn from the *Arthaśāstra* attributed to Kauṭilya that the Vṛishṇis were a *Saṅgha* or 'corporation.' Their political constitution was therefore similar to that of the Śākyas among whom Gautama Buddha was born. Their irreverent attitude towards Brāhmaṇas is alluded to by all our authorities.[7]

In the *Chhāndogya Upanishad* Kṛishṇa is represented as the son of Devakī and a pupil of

1 ii, 11, 9, 3.

2 i, 6, 1.

3 iii, 10, 9, 15.

4 iii, 1, 1, 4.

5 xiii, 5, 4, 21.

6 viii, 14, 3.

7 Kauṭilya, *Arthaśāstra*, 1919, p. 12; *Mahābhārata*, xvi, 15-22; Cowell's *Jātaka*, Vol. IV, pp. 55-56, Vol. V, p. 138.

Ghora Āṅgirasa. The *Ṛishi* Ghora Āṅgirasa was a priest of the sun.[1] The *Chhāndogya* text gives an account of the doctrines which he taught his disciple. In the opinion of the Ṛishi the *Purusha* (man) may be compared to a *yajña* (sacrifice). When the man is hungry, thirsty and enjoys no pleasure his condition corresponds to the *dīkshā* or initiation, when the performer of a sacrifice has to fast and abstain from all worldly pleasure. When he eats, drinks and enjoys himself his condition corresponds to the *upasada* when the sacrificer breaks the fast and takes food. When he laughs, feeds and indulges in pleasure his state corresponds to the *Stutaśastra* when there are music, singing of hymns and the recitation of sacred books. Penance, almsgiving, straightforwardness, harmlessness and truthfulness constitute the fee. When the man is conceived in his mother's womb, people say *soshyati* "The mother will give birth," when the child is born, they say *asoshṭa* "The mother has given birth," these correspond to the use of such expressions in the actual sacrifice. The death of a man corresponds to the final sacrificial bath (*avabhṛitha*).

Having thus explained this subject (*Purusha-yajña Vidyā*) to Kṛishṇa, the son of Devakī, the *Ṛishi* added :—"Let him when his end approaches meditate on these three: 'O Thou art the

[1] Kaush. Br., 30, 6; Hopkins, R. I., p. 466.

Imperishable! Thou art the Unchangeable (or Unfailing)! Thou art the true Essence of Life.' " Hearing this Kṛishṇa is said to have "lost all thirst for other knowledge." The sage then quoted two *Ṛig-Vedic* verses bearing on the subject:

" *Ādit pratnasya retasaḥ*
Udvayantamasaspari jyotiḥ paśyanta uttaraṁ
Svaḥ paśyanta uttaraṁ
Devaṁdevatrā Sūryamaganma jyotiruttamamiti
Jyotiruttamamiti."

"Having beheld the glory of the First Cause—that exquisite light, high above all darkness—and having beheld it also in our own hearts, we attain to that god of gods and noblest of all lights, the Sun—the noblest of all lights." [1]

In the *Upanishad* passage mentioned above Kṛishṇa is associated with a school of thought that rejected the ritualistic interpretation of sacrifice (*Vidhi-yajna*) and gave a new meaning to human life and activities. Man's life is as sacred as a sacrifice and death is merely the final sacrificial bath provided he pays *dakshiṇā* to his fellow beings in the shape of charity, non-violence, truthfulness and other virtues. He should when death approaches him meditate on the Imperishable,

[1] In the *Bhīshmastavarāja* (Mbh. xii, 47, 38-40) Kṛishṇa is described in similar terms by Bhīshma.

the Unfailing, the True Essence of Life and remember the "exquisite light, high above all darkness." Such a man can verily attain to the Sun, god among the gods, the noblest of all lights.

The doctrines which Kṛishṇa learnt from his Guru reappear in the *Gītā* which is attributed to the former. In the *Upanishad* Kṛishṇa learnt that all the acts of life constitute a sort of sacrifice offered to the deities in the case of a man who leads a pious life—a life that enables him to attain to the "god among the gods." With this doctrine we may compare the teaching of the *Gītā*, ix, 27.

Yat karoshi yadaśnāsi
yajjuhoshi dadāsi yat
yat tapasyasi Kaunteya
tatkurushva madarpanam.

In the *Gītā*, iv, 33 Kṛishṇa makes little of *dravyamayayajña* (material sacrifice) as his Guru does of *vidhi-yajña.*

In the *Upanishad* Kṛishṇa learnt that "*Tapodānamārjjavamahiṁsāsatyavachanam*" are as efficacious (*dharmapushṭikara*) as gifts to priests in an ordinary sacrifice. In the *Gītā* he teaches—"*Dānam damaścha yajñaścha svādhyāyam tapa ārjjavam ahiṁsā satyam*" are his who is born to godlike endowments.[1]

[1] Gītā, xvi, 3.

We shall place side by side a few more passages of the *Upanishad*, and the corresponding texts of the *Bhagavadgītā*. It will be seen that Kṛishṇa, like Ghora, emphasises the need of meditation "at the last hour" on the "word which knowers of the Veda call Imperishable" and "the sun-coloured being beyond the darkness," as the best means of attaining to the Supreme Celestial Person.[1]

1. *Antavel āyāmetat trayam pratipadyeta-akshitama-syachyutamasi prāṇ-śaṁsitamasīti.*	1. *Antakāle chamāmeva smaraṇmuktvākalevaram paramaṁpurushaṁdivyaṁ yāti Pārthānuchintayan* —*Gītā, viii*, 5-*8.* *Prayāṇakāle.................* *Yadaksharaṁ vedavido vadanti sayātiparamāṁgatim* —*viii*, *10-13.*
2. *Udvayantamasaspari jyotiḥ paśyanta utta-raṁ svaḥ paśyanta uttaraṁ devaṁdevatrā Sūryamaganma.*	2. *Anusmaredyaḥ sarvasya dhātāramachintya rūpa-mādityavarṇaṁ-tamasaḥ parastāt sataṁparaṁ purushamupaiti divyam* —*viii*, *9-10.*

How are we to account for these coincidences? They cannot be fortuitous. In the *Upanishad* and

1 *Cf.* Hill, *Gītā*; also Mbh., xii, 47, 40, "*Mahatastamasaḥ pāre Purushaṁ hyatitejasam yam jñātvā mṛityumatyeti tasmai jñeyātmane namaḥ* "—*Bhīshmastavarāja.*

in the *Gītā* we find the same doctrines associated with the name of one and the same person (Kṛishṇa, the son of Devakī). There is no escape from the conclusion that these doctrines were actually learnt by Kṛishṇa from Ghora Āṅgirasa, and were transmitted by him to his disciples—the Bhāgavatas—and formed the kernel of the poem known as the *Bhagavadgītā*.

Though the *Gītā* contains the doctrines which Kṛishṇa inherited from his Guru, yet it is by no means a product of the age in which Kṛishṇa lived. Kṛishṇa himself is mentioned in one of the oldest *Upanishads*, while the *Gītā* presupposes the existence of all the classical *Upanishads* by its reference to the *Brahmasūtras*.[1]

Ṛishibhirbahudhāgītam
chhandobhirvividhaiḥ pṛithak
Brahmasūtrapadaiśchaiva
hetumadbhirviniśchitaiḥ.

"Hear and learn from me the Supreme Soul (*Kshetrajña*) that has been celebrated in many ways by *Ṛishis* in various metres, and by the words of the *Brahmasūtras*, which are definite and furnished with reasons."[2] Here the words *Brahmasūtrapadaiḥ* seem to Max Müller to refer clearly to the recognised title of the *Sūtras* of Bādarāyaṇa.

1 *Gītā*, xiii, 5.

2 Max Müller's *Indian Philosophy*, p. 118.

The words "definite and argumentative" can refer to *Sūtras* only. Now as the *Brahmasūtras* refer, by the name of *Śruti*, to the *Bṛihadāraṇyaka*, *Chhāndogya* and other ancient *Upanishads*, the *Gītā* must be considered to be posterior to all these works. Even if the reference, in the *Gītā*, is to an earlier recension of the *Brahmasūtras* long anterior to the extant aphorisms attributed to Bādarāyaṇa, it cannot be denied that the "Lord's song" presupposes the classical *Upanishads*, for it is impossible to conceive of a *Brahmasūtra* however ancient which is not based on those texts.[1]

Several scholars have attempted to fix the date of the *Gītā*. According to Telang "the *Gītā* must have been composed at the latest somewhere about the fourth century B.C."[2] Dr. Macnicol observes in his *Indian Theism*,[3] "the *Gītā* is post-Buddhistic, and at least a considerable part of it is pre-Christian."

The *Gītā* is mentioned in the *Kādambarī* of Bāṇabhaṭṭa, the court-poet of Harshavardhana, who flourished in the first half of the seventh century A.D. In the *Kādambarī* one of the equivoques runs as follows :—

1 Garbe seems to think that the *Gītā* shows acquaintance with the *Kaṭha*, *Śvetāśvatara* and even the *Nṛisiṁha tāpanīya Upanishads* (Introduction to the *Bhagavadgītā* translated by N. B. Utgikar, *Indian Antiquary*, 1918, p. 31).

2 *Introductory Essay to the Bhagavadgītā*, p. xcii.

3 P. 76.

"*Mahābhāratamivānantagītākarṇaṇānanditanaram*" —"(the royal palace) in which people were gratified by hearing innumerable songs was like the *Mahābhārata*, in which Nara (Arjuna) was gratified by hearing the *Anantagītā*."

The testimony of the Khoh Copper-plate Inscription of Śarvanātha carries the proof of the antiquity of the *Gītā* several centuries further back. We learn from that inscription that the *Mahābhārata* in the first half of the sixth century A.D. contained one hundred thousand *ślokas*. As Professor Macdonell points out, it certainly included the twelfth and thirteenth books, and even the supplementary book called the *Harivaṁśa* without any of which it would have been impossible to speak even approximately of one hundred thousand verses. As the *Gītā* is alluded to in the twelfth book[1] it must have existed long before the sixth century A.D. The *Anugītā* which forms part of the fourteenth book of the *Mahābhārata*, also presupposes the existence of the *Bhagavadgītā*. There can be no question that the *Gītā* is one of the older poems of the Great Epic.

The *Gītā* was certainly known to Kālidāsa and the author of the extant *Brahmasūtras*. As pointed out by Mallinātha, Telang and Garbe, the passage in the *Kumārasaṁbhava* of Kālidāsa where Aṅgiras says to Himālaya :

[1] xii, 348, 8, 53.

sthāne tvām sthāvarātmānam
Vishṇum āhur manīshiṇaḥ,[1]

"Rightly do the wisé call thee Vishṇu in the shape of a mountain," we have an unmistakable reference to the *Gītā* x, 25 (*asmi sthāvarāṇāṁ Himālayaḥ*) both in form and in sense. The extant *Brahmasūtras*, when they refer to *Smṛiti*, refer clearly to passages taken from the *Bhagavadgītā* also. Under *Sūtra*, i, 2, 6, Śankara quotes *Gītā* xviii, 61. .Under *Sūtra* ii, 3, 45 all the famous commentators (Śaṅkara, Rāmānuja and Madhva) cite *Gītā*, xv, 7. Again under iv, 2, 22 all these commentators refer to the same passage—that at the close of the *Gītā*, Chap. viii.[2] But as the *Gītā* cetainly appeals to the *Brahmasūtras*[3] this reciprocal quotation according to some scholars might be accounted for by their being contemporaneous.[4] The *Chārudatta* attributed to Bhāsa, a predecessor of Kālidāsa, seems to allude to the *Brahmasūtras*.[5] In his introduction to the sacred laws of Āpastamba Dr. Bühler observes[6] "he (Āpastamba) knew not only the unsystematic speculations contained in the *Upanishads* and *Āraṇyakas*, but a well-defined system of Vedāntic philosophy identi-

1 vi, 67.
2 Telang's *Introductory Essay to the Bhagavadgītā*, p. xci.
3 xiii, 5.
4 Max Müller's *Indian Philosophy*, p. 119.
5 Act III. Ed. by Ganapati Śāstrī, p. 74.
6 P. xxviii.

cal with that of Bādarāyaṇa's *Brahmasūtras.*" The same writer says that "on linguistic grounds Āpastamba cannot be placed later than the third century B.C."[1] If the views of Max Müller and Bühler are accepted then the *Brahmasūtras* as well as the *Bhagavadgītā* must have existed at least as early as the third century B.C. From the absence of any allusion to the *Vyūha* doctrine in the *Gītā* Sir R. G. Bhandarkar concludes that it was earlier than the Ghosuṇḍî and Nānāghāṭ inscriptions and the *Mahābhāshya* of Patañjali (second century B.C.) all of which show acquaintance with the *Vyūhavāda.* Garbe thinks that the mention in the *Gītā* of the word Himālaya, the modern form of the older Himavat, makes an impression of relative lateness. It should however be remembered that *Simalia,* the ancient Babylonian queen of the snow mountains, can hardly be dissociated from the name Himālaya,[2] though it must be conceded that the occurrence of the word Himālaya in Sanskrit literature is comparatively late. An important thing to remember is that the *Gītā* is one of the older poems of an epic which was virtually completed before the beginning of active intercourse with Rome (first century B.C.), for while the *Yavanas* and *Pahlavas* are mentioned very often, the *Romakas* are

[1] P. xliii. A date in the second century B.C. is suggested by Hopkins in the *Cambridge History of India,* Vol. I, p. 249.

[2] *Cambridge History of India,* Vol. I, p. 76.

mentioned but once and we have no reference to the *Denarius* until we come to the supplementary book styled the *Harivamśa*. Hill rightly points out that the *Gītā* was written at a time when the idea of Vāsudeva as supreme was far from meeting with that tolerant acceptance among the orthodox which it afterwards won.[1]

If the extant *Brahmasūtras* show acquaintance with the Buddhist *Vijñānavāda* and *Śūnyavāda* and the Bhāgavata doctrine of the *Vyūhas* as suggested by Śaṅkara, then the *Brahmasūtra* mentioned in the *Gītā* and the aphorisms of Āpastamba must refer to an earlier recension of the work.

The precise extent of Kṛishṇa's own contributions to the doctrines contained in the *Gītā* cannot easily be ascertained. From the importance attached to "*dama, tyāga* and *apramāda*" in the *Bhāgavata* inscription of Heliodoros at Besnagar, one is tempted to infer that these doctrines were believed to have been taught by the Master Himself. "*dama*, and *tyāga*," self-restraint and self-denial are inculcated in the *Gītā*, xvi, 1-2, xviii, 2,51, etc., and *pramāda*, heedlessness, is considered to be the product of *tamas* (darkness) and is classed with those impediments "by crossing beyond which the embodied soul attains *amṛitam*," deathlessness. But these precepts are not to be found in the corresponding passage of the *Chhān-*

[1] *Cf.* Gītā, vii, 19; ix. 11.

dogya Upanishad[1] which embodies the teaching of Ghora Āṅgirasa.

Chh. Up.	Gītā.	Bes. Ins.
Tapodānamārjja-	*Dānam Damaścha*	Trīṇi *amuta*
vam ahiṁsā	yajñaścha	padāni
satyavachanamiti	svādhyāyam *tapa*	suanuṭhitāni
	ārjjavam	nayamtisvaga
	ahiṁsā satyam	*dama chāga*
	akrodha *styāgaḥ*	*apramāda*
	śāntir apaiśunam.	
	Sattvātsaṁjāyate jñānam	
	rajaso lobha eva cha	
	pramāda mohau tamaso	
	bhavato' jñānameva cha	
	guṇānetānatītyatrīn	
	dehīdehasamudbhavān	
	janma mṛityu jarā duḥkhair	
	vimukto' *mṛitamaśnute.*[2]	

We have seen that the *Bhāgavata* religion, the parent of modern *Vaishṇavism*, arose in the Mathurā region, and that its founder was a scion of the *Vṛishṇi* or *Sātvata* branch of the *Yādava* clan and a disciple of the Ṛishi Ghora Āṅgirasa, a priest of the Sun.

There is much truth in Grierson's surmise that the *Bhāgavata* doctrine was a development of the Sun-worship that was the common heritage of both branches of the Aryan people—the Iranian and the Indian.[3] All the legends dealing with the origin of the *Bhāgavata* religion are connected in

[1] *Gītā*, xiv, 17-20; *cf. Chhāndogya*, iii, 17, 4.

[2] *Gītā*, xiv, 17-20.

[3] Ind. Ant., 1908, p. 253.

some way or other with the Sun. According to the *Śānti-parva* of the *Mahābhārata*, the *Sātvata* code had been declared in ancient times by the Sun—*Sātvatam vidhimāsthāya prāk Sūryamukhaniḥsṛitam.*[1] In the *Gītā* the *Bhagavat* says :—

Imaṁ Vivasvate yogaṁ proktavānahamavyayam
Vivasvān Manave prāha Manur Ikshvākave'bravīt.[2]

" To Vivasvat (the Sun) I expounded this immutable doctrine of control ; to Manu did Vivasvat declare it ; Manu told it to Ikshvāku." [3]

It was one of the solar deities, *viz.*, Vishṇu, who became the One God of the *Bhāgavatas.* Vāsudeva's *Garuḍa* (Eagle vehicle) and *Chakra* (discus) are also connected with solar legends.[4] The close connection between Bhāgavatism and Solar worship is also possibly suggested by the Khoh Copper-plate Inscription of Śarvanātha, of A.D. 512-13, which records the grant of a village on the river Tamasā for the purposes of shrines of the *Bhagavat* and of Āditya-bhaṭṭāraka.[5]

We have already noticed the doctrines which Kṛishṇa learnt from the priest of the sun, and which he undoubtedly transmitted to his disciples, as is proved by their reappearance in the *Bhaga-*

1 Mbh., xii, 335, 19.

2 *Gītā*, iv, 1.

3 Hill, *Bhagavadgītā*, 137.

4 Macdonell, *Vedic Mythology*, p. 39.

5 Fleet, *Corpus Inscriptionum Indicarum*, Vol. III, 127.

vadgītā. We have also seen that though the *Gītā* is not the work of Kṛishṇa himself or of any of his contemporaries, yet it has preserved, with certain modifications, the actual teachings of the Master and his Guru inflated no doubt by other sayings traditionally attributed to the former. In the history of *Bhāgavatism* the *Gītā* occupies a position similar to that which the *Dhammachakkappavattana Sutta* occupies in Buddhism. The services rendered by the compiler of the *Bhagavadgītā* to the system of Kṛishṇa finds its closest parallel in what the author of the *Sāṁkhyakārikā* did for the system of Kapila.

It is twice asserted in the *Śānti-parva* of the *Mahābhārata* that the *Bhāgavata*, or *Ekāntika*, religion was the burden of the teaching of the *Gītā* :—

"*Evamesha mahān dharmaḥ sate pūrvaṁ nṛipottama*
Kathito Harigītāsu samāsavidhikalpitaḥ." [1]

"*Samupoḍheshvanīkeshu Kuru Pāṇḍavayormṛidhe*
Arjune vimanaskecha gītā Bhagavatā svayam." [2]

The *Bhagavadgītā* is a work which, in spite of its apparent simplicity, has baffled many commentators and critics.[3] To some it appears full of

[1] Mbh., xii, 346, 11.

[2] Mbh., xii, 348, 8.

[3] See Garbe, Introduction to the *Bhagavadgītā*, translated by Utgikar, pp. 1 ff.; Macnicol, *Indian Theism*, pp. 76 ff. T. Rājagopāla Chariar, *The Vaishnavite Reformers of India*, pp. 44 ff.

contradictions ; to others, it is a patchwork of three or four layers set one above another. To others again the central theme is clear, while the work is full of digressions and repetitions. According to Holtzmann it is a Vishṇuite remodelling of a pantheistic poem ; according to Hopkins it is a Kṛishṇaite version of an old Vishṇuite poem, which in turn was a late *Upanishad* ; according to Deussen it is a late product of the degeneration of the monistic thought of the *Upanishads* representing the period of transition from theism to realistic atheism ; according to Garbe it is the text-book of the *Bhāgavatas* revised in a Vedāntic sense by the Brāhmaṇas ; according to Macnicol it is rightly to be described as an *Upanishad* which, though it has more unity than most of its kind, contains interpolations emphasizing the view of one school or another. The Vaishṇava view is put forward in the *Gītārthasaṁgraha* of Yāmunāchārya. Yāmuna following the ancient oral teaching analysed the work as a consistent exposition of the doctrine of *Bhakti* supplemented by a description of the *Karma* and *Jñāna Yogas* as subordinate to the main theme. The prominent features of the Gītā teaching have been sought to be indicated by Dr. Seal in his *Comparative Studies in Vaishṇavism and Christianity*,[1] and a full summary of the work has been given by Sir R. G.

[1] P. 90.

Bhandarkar in his *Vaisṇavism*. The question of the relation of the *Gītā* to Christianity will be discussed in my next lecture.

The central theme of the *Gītā*, as understood in the light of Ghora's teaching and the *Bhāgavata* inscription of Besnagar, is adoration of Vāsudeva, the god of gods (*devadeva*)[1] whose emblem is the sun-bird *Garuḍa Vainateya*. The way to reach immortality (*amṛitam*), the supreme eternal deathless abode, *paramadhāma*, *para sthāna*, *pada anāmaya*, *sthāna śāśvata*, *svaga*, of the *devadeva*, "the light of lights that overpasses darkness," is not the performance of ordinary material sacrifice (*vidhiyajña*, *dravyamaya yajña*) but a spiritualised sacrifice the most essential element of which is the practice of self-control (*dama*), abandonment of the fruit of every work (*tyāga*) and crossing beyond the three "strands" (*guṇa*), especially "darkness" (*tamas*) which is productive of heedlessness (*pramāda*). "He who with unwavering practice of devotion (*bhaktiyogena*) does me (*Vāsudeva*) service (*sevate*) has crossed beyond the strands, and is fit for Brahman's being. The ground of Brahman am I (*Vāsudeva*), of deathlessness (*amṛita*) immutable, of right everlasting, and of pleasure absolute."[2]

The new religion taught by Kṛishṇa seems to have been first adopted by his tribe, the Yādavas,

[1] *Cf. Gītā*, x, 15; xi, 13.
[2] Hill, *Bhagavad Gītā*, 235.

especially by the Sātvata sept to which the Master himself belonged. In the *Śānti-parva* we often find the name *Sātvata* used as a synonym for *Bhāgavata* without any ethnic signification whatever. In the Tusām Rock Inscription of the fourth or fifth century A.D.[1] an *Āryya-Sātvata-Yogāchāryya* is mentioned.

In the fourth century B.C. the strongest adherents of Vāsudeva were to be found only in the Mathurā region, for we learn from Megasthenes that the people who held Herakles in special honour were the Sourasenoi (Śūrasenas) who possessed two large cities, Methora (Mathurā) and Kleisobora, and through whose country flowed a navigable river called the Jobares (Jumna).[2]

We hear little about the *Bhāgavatas* in the third century B.C. But we have a good deal of information regarding the condition of the sect in the second century B.C. The preference which Aśoka openly avowed for Buddhism, and his active propaganda undoubtedly brought his favourite doctrine to the front in the third century B.C., and pushed the rival creeds to a corner.

It is a noticeable fact that the *Bhāgavatas* are almost wholly ignored in the ancient literary and epigraphic records of the Buddhists in Magadha and the neighbouring provinces, but are constantly mentioned from the time of Pāṇini onwards in

1 Corp. Ins. Ind., Vol. III, p. 270.

2 McCrindle, *Megasthenes and Arrian*, p. 201.

the records, literary and epigraphic, of the Western part of Northern India. The *Aṅguttara Nikāya* mentions the *Ājīvikas*, the *Niganṭhas*, the *Muṇḍa-Sāvakas*, the *Jaṭilakas*, the *Paribbājakas*, the *Magaṇḍikas*, the *Tedaṇḍikas*, the *Aviruddhakas*, the *Gotamakas* and the *Devadhammikas*[1] but never the *Vāsudevakas* and the *Arjunakas*. The Seventh Pillar Edict of Aśoka mentions the Brāhmaṇas, the *Ājīvikas* and the *Niganṭhas* or Jainas, but not the *Bhāgavatas*. There is a solitary reference to *Vāsudevavatikā* and *Baladevavatikā*, *i.e.*, the worshippers of Vāsudeva and Baladeva (Saṅkarshaṇa), in a passage occurring in two Canonical Commentaries known as the *Chulla Niddesa* and *Mahā Niddesa*.[2]

The omission of the *Vāsudevakas* or the *Bhāgavatas* in almost all the early records of the Buddhists in Eastern India is probably due to the fact that they were as yet a local sect confined to the Jumna Valley included among the *Devadhammikas* or some other sect, and little known in Magadha and its neighbourhood, though well known to the people of Gandhāra and parts of Central India. The early canonical literature of the Buddhists took note only of the important Kosalan and Magadhan sects, while the Pillar Edicts

[1] Aṅguttara, III, pp. 276-77, Dialogues of the Buddha, Part I, p. 220.

[2] Sir R. G. Bhandarkar, *Vaiṣnavism, Saivism and Minor Religious Systems*, p. 3.

of Aśoka were intended mainly for the "home provinces" from which the land of the *Bhāgavatas* was presumably excluded. The Niddesa list,[1] on the other hand, apparently originated among the followers of Mahā Kachchāyana who was the first among the chief disciples of Śākyamuni through whose agency Buddhism gained ground in the Mathurā region.[2]

Whatever may have been the state of the *Bhāgavatas* in the third century B.C., we learn from the inscriptions at Ghosuṇḍī and Besnagar that in the second century B.C. the *Bhāgavata* religion had overstepped the boundaries of the Mathurā region and spread to the Indian Borderland, and that its fame had reached the ears of non-Indian peoples some of whom became converts to the faith.

The Ghosuṇḍī Stone Inscription[3] records the erection of a *pūjā stone* wall (*Silāprākāra*) at the Nārāyaṇavāṭa by Sarvatāta Gājāyana, the son of a Pārāśarī, a performer of the *Aśvamedha* sacrifice, for *Bhagavat*, *Sarveśvara* (supreme lord), Saṅkarshaṇa and Vāsudeva.

The worship of Saṅkarshaṇa is alluded to in the *Kauṭilîya Arthaśāstra*. Mention is made in that work of a class of ascetics "with shaved head

1 *Chulla Niddesa*, pp. 173-74. I owe this reference to Dr. Barua.

2 *Vide* the *Madhura Sutta* of the *Majjhima Nikāya*.

3 *Epigraphia Indica*, Vol. X, Appendix, p. 2; xvi, 25; *Indian Antiquary*, 1932, 203 ff.

or braided hair" who adored Saṅkarshaṇa as their *devatā*. In the earlier part of the *Mahābhārata* Saṅkarshaṇa is the elder brother of Kṛishṇa Vāsudeva [1] and his helper in the struggle against Kaṁsa.[2] He is held in special honour by Duryodhana, king of the Kurus, while his brother receives the homage of the Pāṇḍus. In the *Bhîsmaparva* and the *Ahirbudhnya Saṁhitā* Saṅkarshaṇa appears as an exponent of the *Sātvata* or *Pañcharātra śāstra*. In the religious philosophy of Bhāgavatism as expounded in the *Nārāyaṇīya* section of the *Śāntiparva*, Vāsudeva is identified with the *Paramātman* (Supreme Soul), while Saṅkarshaṇa is identified with the individual soul or *Jīva*.

Yaṁ praviśya bhavantīha muktā vai dvija sattamāḥ
Sa Vāsudevo vijñeyaḥ paramātmā sanātanaḥ [3]

Jñeyaḥ sa eva rājendra jîvaḥ Saṅkarshanaḥ prabhuḥ.[4]

In the worship of Saṅkarshaṇa and Vāsudeva we have the germ of the *Vyūha* doctrine of the *Bhāgavatas* or *Pañcharātras*. The doctrine of the Vyūhas is thus stated by Grierson.[5] "The Bhagavat Vāsudeva, in the act of creation produces

1 Mbh., ii, 79, 23.
2 Mbh., ii, 14, 34.
3 Mbh., xii, 339, 25.
4 Mbh., xii, 339, 40.
5 Ind. Ant., 1908, p. 261.

13

from Himself, not only *prakṛiti*, the indiscrete primal matter of the Sāṁkhyas, but also a *Vyūha* or phase of conditioned spirit called Saṅkarshaṇa. From the combination of Saṅkarshaṇa and *prakṛiti* spring *manas*, corresponding to the Sāṁkhya *buddhi* or intelligence, and also a secondary phase of conditioned spirit called Pradyumna. From the association of Pradyumna with *manas* spring the Sāṁkhya *ahaṅkāra* or consciousness, and also a tertiary phase of conditioned spirit known as Aniruddha. From the association of Aniruddha with *ahaṅkāra* spring the Sāṁkhya *Mahābhūtas* or elements with their qualities, and also Brahmā, who, from the elements, fashions the earth and all that it contains."[1]

It should be noted that in the Ghosuṇḍî record which we owe to a horse-sacrificing votary of the

[1] Sir R. G. Bhandarkar points out that the *Gītā* contains no allusion to the *Vyūhas*. It however mentions as *Prakṛitis* of Vāsudeva the five elements, the mind, *Buddhi*, egoism and *Jīva* (vii, 4-5). The three *Prakṛitis*, *Jīva*, mind and egoism were later on personified into Saṅkarshaṇa, Pradyumna and Aniruddha (*Vaiṣṇavism*, pp. 12-13). Patañjali probably alludes to the *Vyūhas* in the passage of the *Mahābhāshya—Janārdanastvātmachaturtha eva*. The first clear enunciation of the *Vyūha* doctrine occurs in the *Nārāyaṇīya* section of the *Śānti Parva* which is older than Śaṅkara and probably also than the *Vishṇu Purāṇa*—(Sir R. G. Bhandarkar's *Vaiṣṇavism*, p. 4, and Dr. Seal's *Comparative Studies in Vaiṣṇavism and Christianity*, p. 30). The earliest *Pañcharātra Saṁhitās* that refer to the Vyūha doctrine may be of a somewhat later date (Schrader, Introduction to the Pañcharātra, pp. 96ff.) The *Nārāyanīya* and the *Samhitās* do not give a consistent account of the Vyūhas. *Cf.* Grierson, *Ind. Ant.*, xxxvii, 1908, pp. 377, 379, including notes, and Schrader, *op. cit.*, 35 ff., 50 ff , 143 ff., 152 ff.

Blessed Ones, Saṅkarshaṇa is not a mere emanation from Vāsudeva, but is styled *Bhagavat* and *Sarveśvara* equally with his more famous brother. Saṅkarshaṇa had undoubtedly his special votaries as is proved by the evidence of Kauṭilya and the story of his relations with Duryodhana narrated in the Great Epic.

We now come to the Besnagar Column Inscription of Heliodoros.[1] It was found on the base of a detached pillar standing to the north-east of Besnagar in the Gwalior territory. The Greek king Antialkidas mentioned in the inscription is supposed to have reigned in the second century B.C.[2]

The first part of the inscription records the erection of a *Garuḍadhvaja* of Vāsudeva, the god of gods, by the *Bhāgavata* Heliodora, the son of Diya (Dion), the Takhkhasilāka (native of Taxila), a *Yona* ambassador, who came from *Mahārāja* Aṁtalikita (Antialkidas) to *Rājan* Kāsiputa Bhāgabhadra the Saviour (*trātāra*), who was prospering in the fourteenth year of his reign :—

Devadevasa Vā(sude)vasa Garuḍadhvaje ayaṁ
kārite i(a) Heliodoreṇa Bhāga
vatena Diyasa putreṇa Takhkhasilākena

1 Vogel, *Garuḍa Pillar of Besnagar*, *Arch. Sur. Ind.*, 1908-09, p. 126. Epigraphia Indica, Vol. X, Appendix, p. 63.

2 V. A. Smith's "A History of Fine Art in India and Ceylon," pp. 65-66.

Yona-dūtena āgatena mahārājasa
Aṁtalikitasa upā(ṁ)tā sakāsam Raño
Kāsi putasa Bhāgabhadrasa trātārasa
vasena (chatu) daseṁnarājena vadhamānasa

The second part of the epigraph runs as follows :—

Trini amuta padāni (su)anuṭhitāni
Nayaṁti svaga dama chāga apramāda

"Three immortal precepts (*lit.*, ' steps ') when practised lead to heaven—self-restraint, renunciation and vigilance."

This inscription is one of the most remarkable epigraphic records ever discovered in India. Its importance in the history of Vaishṇavism can scarcely be overestimated. It proves that the *Bhāgavata* sect existed in the second century B.C., and that the object of their worship was Vāsudeva, " the god of gods." With the epithet *devadeva* applied by Heliodoros to the object of his devotion we may compare the appellation "*devam devatrā*" given to Sūrya in the *Ṛig Vedic* verses quoted by Ghora Āṅgirasa for the instruction of Kṛishṇa Devakīputra. It should be remembered that the same epithet is applied to Kṛishṇa Vāsudeva in the *Gītā*, x, 15 ; xi, 13. The inscription of Heliodoros and that of Sarvatāta at Ghosuṇḍî furnish the first clear indication of the apotheosis of Kṛishṇa. According to Sir George Grierson the deification of Kṛishṇa was an accomplished fact as early as the time of Pāṇini. "Before the time of Pāṇini," says he, "the founder of the *Bhāgavata* religion, as has happened to other similar cases in India, became deified, and under his patronymic of Vāsudeva, he was identified with the *Bhagavat*." But there is nothing in the *Ashṭādhyāyī* of Paṇini to warrant such a conclusion. From the context both Vāsudeva and Arjuna of *Sūtra* iv, 3, 98, are to be understood as Kshatriyas.[1] Hopkins goes so far as to state that in Pāṇini's *Sūtra* they were only objects of such worship as is accorded to most Hindu heroes after death.[2] The epithet *tatrabhavat* is applied to Vāsudeva not in the original *sūtra*, but only in the *Mahābhāshya* of Patañjali (as an alternative suggestion). The fact that Vāsudeva, the longer word, is placed before Arjuna, in violation of the general rule in such cases, only shows that it is the name of one who was an object of greater reverence than Arjuna. It does not necessarily indicate that Vāsudeva was already looked upon as a god in the days of Pāṇini himself, though he must have been regarded as such in the time of the *Kāśikā*, a much later authority.

Even in the fourth century B.C. Vāsudeva, the Indian Herakles mentioned by Megasthenes, does not appear to have been regarded as the god of gods, but only as a demi-god. Megasthenes

1 Weber, Ind. Lit., p. 185n.

2 The Great Epic of India, p. 395n.

merely states that he was "held in special honour" by the Sourasenoi, but nowhere says that he was worshipped as the god of gods. The allusion to his "birth" among the Indians probably shows that he was still regarded as a human hero. "They (the Indians) assert that Herakles was born among them." "Herakles however who is currently reported to have come as a stranger, is said to have been in reality a native of India."[1] It is in the Besnagar and Ghosuṇḍî Inscriptions that we find Vāsudeva exalted to the rank of the Supreme Deity and magnificent temples (*Prāsādottama*) were erected in his honour.[2]

The *Garuḍadhvaja* points to the close connection between Vāsudeva and Solar worship, because *Garuḍa* or *Suparṇa* is connected with Vishṇu and other Sun-gods. In the *Bodhāyana Dharma Sūtra*[3] *Garutmān* is associated with Nārāyaṇa-Vishṇu.

The inscription of Heliodoros shows that the *Garuḍa* standard was not copied from the Roman eagle as contended by V. Smith, but was the recognised emblem of Vāsudeva, the lord of the *Bhāgavatas*, in the second century B.C. The Besnagar record testifies to the proselytizing zeal of the *Bhāgavatas* in the pre-Christian centuries, and shows that their religion was excellent enough

1 McCrindle's Megasthenes and Arrian, pp. 39, 200.

2 See the Besnagar inscription of the time of King Bhāgavata.

3 ii, 5, 24.

to capture the hearts of cultured Greeks, and catholic enough to admit them into its fold.

The second part of the inscription may be compared to the Second Pillar Edict of Aśoka. Furthermore, the three immortal precepts—*dama*, *tyāga* and *apramāda* look like a quotation from the *Gītā*, xvi, 1-2 ; xiv, 17-20 where *dama*, and *tyāga* are inculcated and the necessity of "crossing beyond" *tamas* which produces *pramāda*, emphasised.

There are a few verses in the *Udyoga* and *Strî parvans* of the *Mahābhārata*—the Holy Writ of the worshippers of Kṛishṇa (*Kārshṇa veda*)—which show a closer resemblance to the concluding passage of the inscription of Heliodoros :—

"Self-restraint, self-denial and vigilance—in these is centered immortality (*damastyāgo' pramādaścha eteshvamṛitamāhitam*)."

"Self-restraint, self-denial and vigilance—these are the three horses of Brahman. He who rides on the car of his soul, to which are yoked these horses with the help of reins furnished by good conduct, goes, O king, to the region of Brahma, shaking off all fear of death. He who gives assurance of safety to all beings goes, O king, to the supreme station, the abode (*lit.*, step) of Vishṇu where there is felicity."

Damastyāgo' pramādaścha
te trayo Brahmaṇo hayāḥ

śīlaraśmi samāyuktaḥ
sthito yo mānase rathe
tyāktvāmṛityubhayaṁ rājan
Brahmalokaṁ sa gachchhati.
Abhayaṁ sarvabhūtebhyo
yo dadāti mahipate
sa gachcchati paraṁ sthānaṁ
Vishṇoḥ padamanāmayam.[1]

Much light is thrown on the state of Bhāgavatism in the second century B.C. by the *Māhābhāshya* of Patañjali.[2] Patañjali mentions *Vāsudevavargyaḥ* and *Vāsudevavarginaḥ*, *i.e.*, the followers of Vāsudeva. Like Heliodoros who may have been his contemporary, but unlike Pāṇini, Patañjali looked upon Kṛishṇa Vāsudeva not as a mere Kshatriya but as a specially honoured, perhaps divine, being. Under Pāṇ., iv, 3, 98, he puts forth the alternative suggestion that the word Vāsudeva is the name of the *tatrabhavat* and not of a Kshatriya, *i.e.*, Vāsudeva is to be taken here, in his capacity as a being who receives special (perhaps divine) honours and not in his capacity as a mere Kshatriya ; for in this latter capacity the name comes under the *Sūtra* iv, 3, 99.

[1] Mbh., v, 43, 22 ; 45, 7 ; xi, 7, 23-25 ; Raychaudhuri, JASB, 1922, pp. 269-71 ; PHAI[3], 271n ; *Studies in Indian Antiquities*, pp. 20 ff. Carpenter, *Theism in Mediaeval India*, 137 ; Vidhuśekhara Bhaṭṭāchārya, IHQ, 1932, 610.

[2] Ind. Ant., Vol. III, pp. 14-16.

In the time of Patañjali the story of Kṛishṇa was the subject of dramatic representations, perhaps similar to those connected with the festivals in honour of Bacchus and the mediæval European mysteries. The popularity of the Kṛishṇa-cult was not a little due to those dramatic performances—the prototypes of the modern *Yātrās*.

In the dissertation on *Bahuvrīhi* compounds, Pāṇ, ii, 2, 23, the following occurs in the *Mahābhāshya*—*Saṅkarshaṇadvitīyasyabalam Kṛishṇasya vardhatām*, " May the power of Kṛishṇa, assisted by Saṅkarshaṇa increase." From this it may be gathered that Saṅkarshaṇa was his constant companion and helper—as might have been inferred from their close association in the Ghosūṇḍî Inscription. In the epigraph, however, Saṅkarshaṇa is not a mere " second " (*dvitîya*). He is *sarveśvara* equally with his brother.

Under Pāṇ., *Sūtra* vi, 3, 6, Patañjali quotes " *Janārdanastvātmachaturtha eva* "—" Janārdana with himself as the fourth," as an apparent exception to the rule. The line, according to Sir R. G. Bhandarkar, is probably quoted from an existing poem on Kṛishṇa.

In discussing the evidence, afforded by the *Mahābhāshya*, for the early existence of the drama, Weber notices the fact that the two legends mentioned as the subjects of representation are *Balibandha* and *Kaṁsabadha*, and he points out that, as the first of these subjects is undoubtedly taken from the legend of Vishṇu, it is probably necessary to assume that already Vishṇu and Kṛishṇa stood in a close relationship.[1] Patañjali notices under Pāṇini ii, 2, 34, a verse in which it is stated that musical instruments were sounded in the gatherings at the temples of Rāma and Keśava. Rāma and Keśava are undoubtedly Balarāma (Saṅkarshaṇa) and Kṛishṇa (Vāsudeva). The name "Keśava" applied to Kṛishṇa in this verse clearly indicates that in the second century B.C. he was already identified by the Brāhmaṇas with Nārāyaṇa-Vishṇu, for we learn from the *Bodhāyana-Dharma sūtra* that Keśava was an epithet of Nārāyaṇa-Vishṇu.[2]

The exact period when Kṛishṇa Vāsudeva was first identified with Nārāyaṇa-Vishṇu cannot be ascertained. As Vishṇu is one of the solar deities, it is not altogether improbable that he had, from the first, some connection with the religious movement associated with the name of Kṛishṇa who was himself a disciple of a priest of the Sun. But there is no direct evidence to show that Vishṇu occupied a prominent place in the early *Bhāgavata* Pantheon. An image of the four-armed Vishṇu appears on a 'Mitra coin' of Pañchāla,[3] but there is nothing to show that the king who issued the coin was a *Bhāgavata*, *i.e.*,

[1] J. R. A. S., 1908, p. 172.

[2] Bodh. Dh. S., ii, 5, 24.

[3] Cunningham, Coins of Ancient India, p. 84.

an adherent of the Vāsudeva-Saṅkarshaṇa cult. Vishṇu worship may have been a rival Brāhmaṇical cult. A clear indication of the identification of Vāsudeva with Nārāyaṇa-Vishṇu is, however, found in the *Taittirīya Āraṇyaka*,[1] but the date of the work is uncertain. The last book in which the name of Vāsudeva occurs is admittedly a later addition. It is described as *Khilarūpa* or supplementary.[2] According to Dr. Mitra it belongs to the same age with the earliest of the *Tantras*, *i.e.*, at best the beginning of the Christian era. But, as its existence is presupposed by Āpastamba, we are disposed to agree with Dr. Keith that the Āraṇyaka probably dates from the third century B.C.[3] The appearance of Vāsudeva as a name of Nārāyaṇa-Vishṇu in a Brāhmaṇical work of the third century B.C. is significant. Was it the active propaganda of Aśoka that led the Vedic priests to identify Vāsudeva with Nārāyaṇa-Vishṇu for the purpose of winning over the *Bhāgavatas* as their allies ?

The *Mahābhārata* contains indications that it was with great difficulty that the orthodox Brāhmaṇists could be prevailed upon to recognise Kṛishṇa-Vāsudeva as the God Nārāyaṇa Himself.

1 x, 1, 6.

2 See Dr. R. L. Mitra's Introduction to the *Taittirīya Āraṇyaka*, p. 8.

3 J. R. A. S., 1915, p. 840.

In the *Gītā*[1] Kṛishṇa laments that the man of great soul who says 'Vāsudeva is All,' is very hard to find. "Fools scorn me," he adds, "when I dwell in human form." In the reviling scene in the *Sabhāparva* we have the reminiscence of an age when the claim of Kṛishṇa to divine honours was openly denied because he did not happen to be a Brāhmaṇa.[2] In *Mbh.*, i, 197, 33, Vāsudeva is only a hair of Nārāyaṇa. In i, 228, 20, he is identified with Nārāyaṇa, but this Nārāyāṇa is a *Ṛishi*, not the Deity. The identification with the god Nārāyaṇa-Vishṇu was however universally recognised when the epic was complete.[3]

Why was Kṛishṇa identified with Vishṇu and not with any other Vedic god? Here, in seeking to answer this question, there is full scope for the play of conjecture. The following facts seem to be indisputable. Vishṇu was connected from the earliest Vedic times with a work of deliverance for mankind in distress.[4] He is always lauded as a great benefactor of mankind. He shows a disposition which is benevolent to all. He traversed the earth for a dwelling which he was desirous of bestowing on the primeval Man (*Manushe daśasyan*). The men who praise him are secure. Therefore he is lauded by the weak. He assumes different

[1] vii, 19; ix, 11.

[2] ii, 42, 6.

[3] *Cf. Vanaparva*, 189, *Bhīsmastavarāja* (93-94, 99-100).

[4] Rig Veda, vi, 49, 13.

forms in battle.[1] He is the unconquerable preserver who maintained *Dharma*.[2] In the *Śatapatha Brāhmaṇa*[3] we have the remarkable statement that "men are Vishṇus." In the *Aitareya Brāhmaṇa* and several other Vedic texts Vishṇu figures as the great helper of the gods against the Asuras. He assumed the form of a dwarf in order to recover the earth for the gods from the Asuras.[4] All these characteristics of Vishṇu eminently fitted him to be the centre of the *Avatāra* theory propounded in the *Bhagavadgītā*, iv, 8 :—

Paritrāṇāya sādhūnāṁ vināśāya cha dushkṛitām
Dharmasaṁsthāpanārthāya sambhavāmi yuge yuge.

Was the Brāhmaṇic identification of Vāsudeva with Nārāyaṇa-Vishṇu accepted by the *Bhāgavatas* in the pre-Christian centuries, or ignored by them as the Buddhists ignored the identification of their Master with the same deity ? The name of Nārāyaṇa-Vishṇu is conspicuous by its absence in the Bhāgavata inscriptions of the second century B.C. It is Vāsudeva and Saṅkarshaṇa, and not Vishṇu-Nārāyaṇa, who receive the homage of the faithful. The name Nārāyaṇavāṭa, applied to the village or spot mentioned in the Ghosūṇḍī inscription in which the *pūjā* stone wall in honour

[1] *Rig Veda*, vii, 100, 1-6.
[2] *Rig Veda*, i, 22, 18.
[3] v, 2, 5, 2-3.
[4] Śat. B., 1, 2, 5, 5; T. B., 1, 6, 1, 5.

of Saṅkarshaṇa and Vāsudeva was built, does not necessarily prove any connection between the worship of Nārāyaṇa and the cult of Saṅkarshaṇa and Vāsudeva in the second century B.C.

In the *Gītā*, which, says Barth, contains probably the oldest dogmatic exposition we possess of Vishṇuism, Vāsudeva, indeed, says, "I am Vishṇu among the Ādityas," but he says in the same breath, "I am Śaṅkara among the Rudras," so the passage does not prove any special connection between Vāsudeva and Vishṇu. It should also be noted that Vishṇu is here only an Āditya, and not the 'god of gods.' In two other passages Vāsudeva is addressed as Vishṇu, but he is also styled *Maheśvara,* an epithet that is usually found in connection with Śiva.[1] Vāsudeva is never addressed as Nārāyaṇa in the extant *Gītā*.

The *Garuḍadhvaja* of the Besnagar inscriptions, however, undoubtedly points to the recognition by the *Bhāgavatas* of Vāsudeva's connection with Nārāyaṇa-Vishṇu. For we learn from the *Bodhāyana Dharmasūtra* that Garutmān was intimately associated with that deity. As pointed out by Barnett the verse in the inscription of Heliodoros about "three immortal steps" (*trini amuta padāni*), as leading to *svaga* (heaven) sounds like

[1] *Gītā*, xi, 24, 30; v, 29; ix, 11; x, 3; xiii, 22.

an attempt to moralise the old mythical feature of the three steps of Vishṇu.[1]

Here it may be pointed out that although Nārāyaṇa and Vishṇu are regarded as one and the same deity in the *Bodhāyana Dharma Sūtra*, the *Taittirīya Āraṇyaka* and several passages of the *Mahābhārata*[2] they were originally names of distinct deities. We have already seen that Vishṇu is mentioned as early as the *Ṛig-Veda*. He is called in the hymns *Gopā*, *Śipivishṭa*, *Urukrama*, etc., but not Nārāyaṇa. We find the name Nārāyaṇa for the first time in the *Śatapatha Brāhmaṇa*[3] where, however, the deity in question is not in any way *identified* with Vishṇu or any of the Ādityas.

"Prajāpati once upon a time spoke unto Purusha Nārāyaṇa, 'offer sacrifice! offer sacrifice!' He spoke, 'verily, thou sayest to me 'offer sacrifice! offer sacrifice!' and thrice I have offered sacrifice: by the morning service the Vasus went forth, by the midday service the Rudras and by the evening service the Ādityas; now I have but the offering place, and on the offering place I am sitting."

In the thirteenth book Purusha Nārāyaṇa is mentioned as having performed a *Pañcharātra Sattra* (sacrifice continued for five days) and thereby obtaining superiority over all beings and becoming

1 *Hindu Gods and Heroes*, 89.

2 i, 33, 12; xii, 64, 7-8, etc.

3 xii, 3, 4, 1: xiii, 6, 1.

all beings. The name *Pañcharātra* applied to the Bhāgavata sect or to one of its important branches, has, in the opinion of some scholars, reference to this *sattra* of Nārāyaṇa.

In the *Taittirīya Āraṇyaka*[1] Nārāyaṇa appears as "the Deity Eternal, Supreme, and Lord," and receives the name of Hari.

The great Epic gives different accounts of Nārāyaṇa. In certain passages he is called an ancient *Ṛishi*[2] or Seer, the son of Dharma, commonly connected with Nara.[3] Nara and Nārāyaṇa are usually identified with Arjuna and Vāsudeva.[4] In a passage of the *Śāntiparva* of the *Māhābhārata*,[5] however, Kṛishṇa is distinguished from Nārāyaṇa.

The following stories are told about the *Ṛishi* Nārāyaṇa :—

(1) Once Bṛihaspati and Uśanas went to Brahman, and also the Maruts with Indra, the Vasus with Agni, the Ādityas, the Sādhyas, the Seven Ṛishis, the Gandharva Viśvāvasu, the *gaṇas* of Apsarases, and having bowed down to Brahman they sat around him. Just then the two ancient *Ṛishis*, Nara and Nārāyaṇa, left the place.

1 x, 11, 1.

2 The *Rishi* Nārāyaṇa was the "Seer" of the *Purusha Sūkta* of the *Rig Veda*.

3 Mbh., v, 49, 5-20; vii, 200, 57.

4 1, 228, 18; v, 49, 19; etc.

5 xii, 334, 18.

Bṛihaspati said to Brahman: "Who are these two that leave the place without worshipping thee?" Brahman said that they were Nara and Nārāyaṇa who had come from the world of men to the world of Brahman; worshipped by the gods and the Gandharvas they exist only for the destruction of the Asuras. Indra went to the spot where those two were practising austerities, accompanied by all the gods headed by Bṛihaspati. At that time the gods had been very much alarmed in consequence of a war with the Asuras. Indra obtained the boon that Nara and Nārāyaṇa assisted him in the battle. Both of them, by their acts, enjoy numerous eternal and celestial regions, and are repeatedly born in the times of war.[1]

(2) Nārāyāṇa is older than the oldest ones (*pūrveshāmapi pūrvajaḥ*). For some purpose that Creator of the universe took his birth as the son of Dharma. On Himavat (*Śiśiragiri*) he underwent austerities for sixty-six thousand years, and then for twice that period, and thus he became a Brāhmaṇa (*Brahmabhūto*) and beheld the Supreme Deity Śiva. The lotus-eyed Nārāyaṇa recited a hymn to Mahādeva. Śiva then granted him boons, that neither gods, nor the *Asuras*, the *Mahoragas*, the *Piśāchas*, the *Gandharvas*, men, the *Rākshasas*, the birds, the *Nāgas*, nor any creatures should ever be able to withstand his prowess, 'thou shalt

[1] Mbh., v, 49, 2-22.

be superior to myself if thou ever goest to battle with me! ' That god walked over the earth (as Kṛishṇa Vāsudeva), beguiling the universe by his illusive power. From the austerities of Nārāyaṇa was born a great *muni* (sage) Nara, who was equal to Nārāyaṇa himself. Arjuna was none else than that Nara. The two *Ṛishis* or seers who are said to be older than the oldest gods, take their births in every *Yuga* for the benefit of the world.[1]

(3) In the *Kṛita* Age, during the epoch of the self-born Manu, the eternal Nārāyaṇa, the soul of the universe, took birth as the son of Dharma in a quadruple form, namely, as Nara, Nārāyaṇa, Hari and the self-create Kṛishṇa. Amongst them all Nara and Nārāyaṇa underwent the severest austerities by repairing to the Himālayan retreat known by the name of Badari.[2]

In certain other passages of the Great Epic, Nārāyaṇa is the name of a god usually identified with Vishṇu, and not associated with Nara. The god Nārāyaṇa took away the *amṛita* or ambrosia from the Asuras and made Garuḍa his vehicle and emblem.

In the episode of the *Śvetadvīpa* Nārāyaṇa is the name of the strange God of the White Islanders.[3] "On the northern shores of the ocean of milk there is an island of great splendour called

1 Mbh., vii, 200, 57-58.

2 Mbh., xii, 334, 9-10.

3 Mbh., xii, 336, 27-55.

by the name of White Island. The men that inhabit that island have complexions as white as the rays of the moon and are devoted to Nārāyaṇa." "Incapable of being seen, in consequence of his dazzling effulgence, that illustrious Deity can be beheld only by those persons that in course of long ages succeed in devoting themselves wholly and solely to Him."

Sir R. G. Bhandarkar takes Nārāyaṇa to mean the resting place or goal of *Nāra* or a collection of *Naras*, and says that this god has a cosmic character and is not a historical or a mythological individual. This idea of Nārāyaṇa was developed in the period of the *Brāhmaṇas* and the *Āraṇyakas* till at last this god was raised to the dignity of the Supreme Soul.[1] It is, however, significant that Nārāyaṇa is described as a thousand-rayed deity (*sahasrārchisham devam*). The "sea of milk" which laves the White Island (*Śveta dvīpa*), his inaccessible abode and the blessed resort of his favoured votaries, reminds one of the well of honey (*madhva utsa*) in the highest station (*pade parame*) of Vishṇu where pious men rejoice. The strange denizens of the "White Island" who have no organs of senses (*anindriyā*) and yet lick with their tongues, the God of sun-like brightness (*Sūrya-prakhyam*)[2] have a surprising likeness

1 Vaiṣṇavism, pp. 30-31.

2 Mbh., xii, 335, 11; 336, 29; *Rig Veda*, i, 154-5.

with the perfect being of the *Gītā*[1] who is *sarvendriya guṇābhāsa sarvendriya vivarjita*—seeming to possess the functions of all the senses, yet void of all the senses and is the light of lights that overpasses darkness. Clearly Nārāyaṇa and his votaries have solar associations.

Whatever might have been the attitude of the *Bhāgavatas* towards Nārāyaṇa and Vishṇu in the age of the *Taittirīya Āraṇyaka*, it is certain that unlike the Buddhists, they ultimately did accept the identification of their master with these deities, as is evident not only from the Garuḍa Pillar Inscriptions but from the *Nārāyaṇīya*, the Tusām Rock Inscription, and the epigraphic records of the *Paramabhāgavata* emperors of the Gupta line.

Besides the inscriptions discovered at Ghosūṇḍî and Besnagar, and the *Mahābhāshya* of Patañjali, we have another valuable record which testifies to the growing importance of Bhāgavatism in the period immediately preceding the Christian era. This is the famous Nānāghāṭ[2] Cave Inscription.[3] It records, after an invocation of Dha(r)mma, Ida (Indra), Saṅkarshaṇa, and Vāsudeva, the "descen-

[1] xiii, 14.

[2] Nānāghāṭ is a pass in the Western Ghāṭs halfway between Punā and Nāsik.

[3] Lüders, inscription No. 1112, *Epigraphia Indica*, Vol. X, Appendix, p. 121.

dants" of Chandra,[1] the four *Lokapālas* Yama, Varuṇa, Kuvera, and Vāsava, the fees given at various sacrifices by the daughter of the Mahāraṭhi Kalalāya, the scion of the Aṁgiya family, the wife of a king who is called Lord of Dakshiṇāpatha, the mother of the princes Vedasiri, and Sati sirimata.

This inscription is remarkable in many respects. It is not a *Bhāgavata* record like the inscriptions discovered at Besnagar. The reference to sacrificial fees paid to priests for the performance of sacrifices proves incontestably that the donor was a Brāhmaṇist. The deities mentioned are mostly Brāhmaṇic. The appearance among them of the names of Saṅkarshaṇa and Vāsudeva shows that a *rapprochement* between the Brāhmaṇists and the Bhāgavatas had already begun. Such a *rapprochement* is also suggested by the Ghosuṇḍî record which refers to the reverence paid to Saṅkarshaṇa and Vāsudeva by a performer of the horse-sacrifice (*aśvamedha*) which is a Brāhmaṇic rite. The older attitude of the orthodox school towards Vāsudeva is reflected in the reviling scene of the *Sabhāparva* of the *Mahābhārata* :—[2]

[1] Or Chandra and " Sūrya " (not Suta, IHQ, 1931, 412).

[2] 42, 6.

Yadyayaṁ jagataḥ kartā yathainaṁ mūrkha manyase
Kasmānna Brāhmaṇaṁ samyagātmānamava-
gachchhati.

In Mbh., ix, 60, 23, Vāsudeva is painted as a pious hypocrite (*cf. Dharmachchhalamapi śrutvā Keśavāt sa viśāmpate*).

The newer attitude is reflected in the passages where Vāsudeva is represented as a friend of the Brāhmaṇas [1] (*Namo Brahmaṇyadevāya go Brāhmaṇa hitāyacha*), the origin of the Vedas [2] (*Brahmaṇo-mukham*). Persons conversant with the Vedas know Him as Vishṇu [3] (*Purushaṁ sanātanaṁ Vishṇuṁ yaṁ taṁ Vedavido viduḥ*).

The Nānāghāṭ Inscription shows further that the Bhāgavata religion was no longer confined to Northern India, but had spread to the south and had captured the hearts of the sturdy people of Mahārāshṭra. From Mahārāshṭra it was destined to spread to the Tamil country and then flow back with renewed vigour to the remotest corners of the Hindu world.

[1] xii, 47, 94. *Cf. Brahmabhūto*, vii, 200, 61.
[2] xii, 210, 9.
[3] xii, 210, 10.

LECTURE III

BHĀGAVATISM AND THE NON-BRĀHMAṆICAL CREEDS OF ANCIENT INDIA

While the Religion of Vāsudeva was slowly spreading from its cradle in the valley of the Jumna, India saw the rise and progress of three great non-Brāhmaṇical creeds which had chequered careers in the annals of Hindusthān. These were the religions of Makkhali Gosāla, of Vardhamāna Mahāvīra, and of Gautama Buddha. The followers of these faiths were known as *Ājīvikas*, *Nirgranthas* or *Jainas*, and *Saugatas* or *Bauddhas* respectively. A foreign religion, Christianity, was also introduced, probably as early as the third century A.D.

The question of the relation of Bhāgavatism to these religions is a subject well worth study.

Bhāgavatism and the Ājīvikas.

Kern and Bühler were of opinion that the *Ājīvikas* were a subdivision of the *Bhāgavatas*. The *Ājīvikas* acknowledged as their first teacher Nanda Vachchha; in the *Purāṇas* this epithet, "the child of Nanda," is applied to Kṛishṇa Vāsudeva. Utpala in commenting on a passage in the *Bṛihajjātaka* of Varāhamihira which mentions the *Ājīvikas* together with the *Vṛiddhaśrāvakas*, *Nirgranthas*, etc., says :—*Ājīvika grahaṇam cha Nārāyaṇāśritāṇām*—" and the use of *Ājīvika* refers to those who have taken refuge with Nārāyaṇa," and in support of his explanation brings forward two passages which he ascribes to Kālakāchāryya. The first of the passages shows the use of *Ekadaṇḍin* for Ājīvika, the second passage Utpala renders by *Keśava mārga dīkshita Keśavabhaktaḥ Bhāgavataḥ ityarthaḥ*.

Dr. Bühler[1] observes that the recovery of the *Vaikhānasa Dharma sūtra* permits him fully to prove the correctness of Kern's identification of the *Ājīvikas* with the *Bhāgavatas*.

The theory of Kern and Bühler has been plausibly controverted by Prof. D. R. Bhandarkar.[2] He says that the real meaning of the extract from Utpala's commentary has been misunderstood by Kern and Bühler. Utpala does not say that the word *Ājīvika* means *Nārāyaṇāśrita*. He merely says that in the text on which he is commenting the word *Ājīvika* is used as an *Upalakshaṇā* to denote *Nārāyaṇāśrita*. *Upalakshaṇā* means a mark indicative of something that the word itself does not actually express. The view of Bhandarkar is now generally accepted by scholars.[3]

1 J. R. A. S., 1911, p. 960.

2 The *Indian Antiquary*, 1912, pp. 286, *et seq.*

3 *Cf.* V. Smith's *Early History of India*, Third Edition, p. 166 n.

Bhāgavatism and Jainism.

The Jainas represent Vāsudeva as a near relation of the *Arhat* Aristanemi.[1] They include Vāsudeva and Baladeva among the sixty-three *Śalākā-Purushas.*[2] The *Śalākā-Purushas* are the great personages who, according to the belief of the Jainas, have, since the present order of things, risen in the history of the world, and directed or influenced its course ; they comprise the twenty-four *Tīrthankaras*, the twelve *Chakravartins*, the nine Vāsudevas, the nine Baladevas, and the nine Prativāsudevas. The first Jaina *Upāṅga* called the *Aupapātika Sūtra* mentions Baladevā and Vāsudevā, and cites two ancient *Ślokas* or verses where eight *Kshatriya* teachers are mentioned, sharply distinguished from eight Brāhmaṇa *parivvāyā* (wandering friars). Among the former we find the name of Bala Rāma. The *Ślokas* containing the lists of teachers are given below :—

" *tattha khalu ime aṭṭha māhaṇa-*
parivvāyā bhavanti, taṁ jahā :

Kaṇṇe ya Karakaṇṭe ya
Ambaḍe ya Parāsare
Kaṇhe Dīvāyaṇe ceva
Devagutte ya Nārae ;

1 Uttarādhyayana, Lec. xxii.

2 Hemachandra's Trishashṭiśalākā-purusha-charita ; Rādhākānta Deva's Sabdakalpadruma, p. 1492 ; Jacobi's Sthavirāvalīcharita, p. 3 ; Barth, Religions of India, p. 167 n.

tattha khalu ime aṭṭha khattiya-
parivvāyā bhavanti, taṁ jahā :

Sīlāī Masiṁ hāre
Naggaī Bhaggaī tiya
Videhe Rāyā Rāme Bale tiya.[1]

It will be remembered in this connection that in the *Bhīsma Parvan* of the *Mahābhārata* the *Sāttvata-vidhi* (the code of the Sātvatas or Bhāgavatas) is said to have been sung by Saṅkarshaṇa (Balarāma) :

Sāttvataṁ vidhim āsthāya
gîtaḥ Saṅkarshaṇena yaḥ
Dvāparasya yugaṣhyānte
ādau Kaliyugasya cha.

In the *Ahirbudhnya Saṁhitā*, too, the original *Śāstra* of the *Pañcharātra* sect "which, at the beginning of the golden age, came down from heaven like a thunder-clap, dispelling all inner darkness," is stated to have been proclaimed by Saṅkarshaṇa.[2]

In the *Chhāndogya Upanishad* Ghora Āṅgirasa while instructing his disciple Kṛishṇa Devakîputra placed certain moral states on an equality

1 *Aupapātika Sūtra*, edited by Dr. Ernst Leumann, pp. 61, 69-70.

2 Schrader, *Introduction to the Pāñcarātra and the Ahirbudhnya Saṁhitā*, pp. 15, 108.

with certain parts of the sacrificial procedure. Among these moral states *Ahiṁsā* is specially mentioned. The *Ahiṁsā* doctrine foreshadowed here was taken up by the Jainas.

In the opinion of Dr. Keith[1] "the (Jaina) faith is deeply permeated with Hindu influences, and especially with influences of Kṛṣṇa worship." "Of this there can be no more striking proof than the taking over of the Kṛṣṇa legend and its reworking in a tedious shape; its importance is seen in the fact that the legend of Mahāvīra's birth is entirely derived from that of Kṛṣṇa's birth."[2]

Dr. Macnicol observes:[3] "in its original democratic character and in its universalism, we have two notes of theism which the sect of Mahāvīra may have learned from such worship as that of Vāsudeva-Kṛishṇa."

Bhāgavatism and Buddhism.

We now come to the important question of *Bhāgavata* influence on Buddhism. We have already stated that the story of Vāsudeva forms the subject of one of the Buddhist *Jātakas, viz.*, the *Ghata Jātaka.* Ghata, the brother of Vāsudeva,

1 J.R.A.S., 1915, pp. 842-843.

2 *Cf.* Jacobi, Jaina Sūtras, Part I, S.B.E., Vol. XXII, pp. 218-230, and Vishṇu Purāṇa, v, 1, 72 *et seq.*

3 *Indian Theism*, p. 63.

is identified with the Buddha himself, while Vāsudeva is identified with Sāriputta.[1]

There can be no doubt of the immense influence which Bhāgavatism exercised upon Buddhism. The *Ahiṁsā* doctrine foreshadowed in the *Chhāndogya Upanishad* was afterwards taken up by the Buddhists as well as the Jainas. The *Saddharmapuṇḍarīka* contains a number of passages which remind us of the *Gītā*. In *Saddharma*, xv, 7-9, Buddha says : "Repeatedly am I born in the world of the living......... I see how the creatures are afflicted......... I will reveal to them the true law." This looks like an echo of the *Gītā*, iv, 7-8, "Whensoever piety languishes, and impiety is in the ascendant, I create myself. I am born age after age, for the protection of the good, for the destruction of evil-doers, and the establishment of piety."

The *Mahāyānaśraddhotpāda* (Awakening of Faith), attributed to the famous Buddhist writer Aśvaghosha, also shows abundant traces of the influence of the *Bhagavadgītā*. Teitaro Suzuki, the translator of the *Awakening of Faith*, observes[2] : "A supplementary point to be noticed in Aśvaghosha is the abundance of similar thoughts and passages with those in the *Bhagavadgītā*." The same writer adds that "it is an open question which of the two has an earlier date." But a

1 Cowell's *Jātaka*, Vol. IV, p. 57.

2 P. 44.

comparison of the styles of Aśvaghosha's *Buddhacharita* and of the *Bhagavadgītā* leaves no room for doubt that the *Gītā* preceded Aśvaghosha. The *Gītā* belongs to an age considerably prior to the epoch of the artificial *Kāvya* literature to which the *Buddhacharita* belongs. In its general character, the style impresses one as quite archaic in its simplicity. It is considered by a critic like Hopkins to be one of the older poems of the *Mahābhārata*. We have adduced reasons for believing that it was probably composed before the Christian era, whereas "by the unanimous testimony of the best authorities we yet have on the later forms of Buddhism, that is to say, the Tibetan and Chinese historiographers, Aśvaghosha lived in the time of the most famous of the Kushān kings, Kanishka."[1] Aśvaghosha alludes to numerous episodes of the *Mahābhārata* including the *Harivaṁśa*.[2] That he was fairly acquainted with the Kṛishṇa story is proved by his reference to the famous deeds of Śauri (Kṛishṇa) which his ancestors who were mere warriors were unable to perform :—

Āchāryyakaṁ yogavidhau dvijānām
aprāptamanyair Janako jagāma
khyātāni karmāṇi cha yāni Śaureḥ
Śūrādayasteshvabalābabhūvuḥ.[3]

1 Rhys Davids, *Buddhist India*, pp. 314-15.

2 Raychaudhuri, *Studies in Indian Antiquities*, pp. 173f.

3 Buddhacharita, Canto I, 50.

"Janaka attained a power of instructing the twice-born in the rules of *yoga* which none other had ever reached; and the famed feats of the grandson of Śūra (Kṛishṇa) Śūra and his peers were powerless to accomplish."[1]

In the *Gītā*[2] Kṛishṇa says: "I am immortality and also death; and I, O Arjuna! am that which is and that which is not." In the *Awakening of Faith* we have the following passage:—"The Soul as birth-and-death comes forth from the Tathāgata's womb. But the immortal (*i.e.*, suchness) and the mortal (*i.e.*, birth-and-death) coincide with each other."[3]

Aśvaghosha says[4] that "After this reflection they should make great vows (*mahāpraṇidhāna*), and with full concentration of spiritual powers think of the Buddha and the *Bodhisattvas*. When they have such a firm conviction, free from all doubts, they will assuredly be able to be born in the Buddha country beyond, when they pass away from the present life, and seeing there Buddhas and Bodhisattvas, to complete their faith and to eternally escape from all evil creations (*apāya*)." The same idea of salvation, says Suzuki, is expressed in the *Bhagavadgītā*:[5] "He who leaves this

1 The Buddhacharita of Aśvaghosha, translated by E. B. Cowell, p. 50.

2 ix. 19.

3 Teitaro Suzuki's translation, pp. 60-61.

4 *Op. cit.*, p. 145.

5 viii. 5-7.

body and departs (from this world) remembering me in (his) last moments, comes into my essence. There is no doubt of that. Also whichever form (of deity) he remembers when he finally leaves this body, to that he goes, O son of Kuntī! having been used to ponder on it. Therefore, at all times remember me, and engage in battle. Fixing your mind and understanding on me, you will come to me, there is no doubt."

Dr. Macnicol agrees with Senart that "the Buddhist tradition certainly moves in a Kṛishṇaite atmosphere."[1] Senart and Poussin are of opinion that there was an intimate relation between the new way of deliverance and the old theistic cults of India, and affirm with confidence that devout worshippers of Nārāyaṇa had much to do in the making of the Buddhist doctrine even from its inception.[2] Mr. Jayaswāl points out[3] that the custom of worshipping footprints had been already an old institution before the time of the Buddha. It probably originated in the Vedic legend of Vishṇu's stepping over the earth, and was borrowed by the Buddhists. In the opinion of Mr. Jayaswāl Aurṇavābha, a predecessor of Yāska, takes the verse '*idaṁ Vishṇur vichakrame tredhā nidadhe padam*' in the sense that Vishṇu literally and physically in the past strode in the manner

[1] *Indian Theism*, p. 65.

[2] Poussin's *Opinions*, pp. 241-8.

[3] Ind. Ant., 1918, March, p. 84.

described by Śākapūni, stepping over the earth, horizon and sky, and "in ascending (he stepped) at the Vishṇupada on the Gayā peak" (*Samārohaṇe Vishṇupade Gayaśirasītyaurṇavābhaḥ*). The passage has, however, been interpreted differently by Durgāchārya. According to Durga Aurṇavābha says, "He (Vishṇu) plants one foot on the *Samārohaṇa* (ascension); (another) on the *Vishṇupada*, the meridian sky; (a third) on the *Gayaśiras*, the hill of setting."[1]

Bhāgavatism and Christianity.

The appearance in India of a religion of *Bhakti* was, in the opinion of several eminent Western scholars, an event of purely Christian origin. Christianity, according to these scholars, exercised an influence of greater or less account on the worship and story of Kṛishṇa.

P. Georgi in his *Alphabetum Tibetanum* stated that '*Krishṇu*' is only "a corruption of the name of the Saviour; the deeds correspond wonderfully with the name, though they have been impiously and cunningly polluted by most wicked impostors." He supposed that the borrowing took place from the "apocryphal books concerning Jesus Christ," and especially from the Manichaeans. But even Weber was forced to admit that his proofs were very wild. He derived the names Ayodhyā,

1 Muir, *Original Sanskrit Texts*, Vol. IV, Ch. 2.

Yudishṭhira, Yādava, from Juda, Arjuna from John, Durvāsas from Peter.[1]

Sir William Jones went the length of asserting[2] that "the spurious gospels which abounded in the first ages of Christianity, had been brought to India, and the wildest part of them repeated to the Hindus, who ingrafted them on the old fable of Cesava, the Apollo of Greece."

Polier,[3] sought at least in the victory over Kāliya, "a travesty of the tradition of the Serpent, the tempter who introduces death into the world, and whose head the Saviour of the human race shall crush."

Kleuker, in his treatise on the history and the antiquities of Asia, says that he can believe that the Kṛishṇa story did not take its origin from the Gospels, but it is quite possible that it has borrowed something from them.

In later times there were, we are told, special theological reasons unfavourable to the discussion of the question of the indebtedness of Kṛishṇaism to Christianity. Writers seemed to fear that some of the sanctity of Christianity would be lost if something borrowed from it was found in the Kṛishṇa cult.

The discussion of the question was revived by Weber, the great German writer, in his essay, "An

1 The *Indian Antiquary*, 1874, 21 ff.

2 As. Res., i, 274.

3 *Mythologie*, i, 445.

investigation into the origin of the festival of Kṛishṇa *Janmāsṭamī*."[1] Weber's theory of the indebtedness of Kṛishṇaism to Christianity rests on the following points[2] :—

(1) The worship of Kṛishṇa as sole God is one of the latest phases of Indian religious systems, of which there is no trace in Varāhamihira.

(2) This worship of Kṛishṇa as sole God has no intelligible connection with his earlier position in the Brāhmaṇical legends. In the *Chhāndogya Upanishad* Kṛishṇa is an "eager scholar." In the *Mahābhārata* he is a brave hero and warrior of the Vṛishṇi race. But in the same epic he appears further exalted to semi-divine rank as the wise friend and counsellor of the Pāṇḍavas, of supernatural power and wisdom. There is a gap between the earlier and later positions of Kṛishṇa which nothing but the supposition of an external influence can açcount for.

(4) The legend, in the *Mahābhārata*, of *Śveta-dvīpa* and the revelation which is made there to Nārada by *Bhagavat* Himself shows that Indian tradition bore testimony to such an influence.

(5) The legends of Kṛishṇa's birth, the solemn celebration of his birthday, in the honours of which his mother Devakī participates, and finally his life as a herdsman, a phase the furthest

1 *Indian Antiquary*, 1874.

2 Ind. Ant., 1873, p. 285; Ind. Ant., 1874, "*Weber on the Kṛishṇa Janmāsṭamī*."

removed from the original representation, can only be explained by the influence of Christian legends.

As to the first point, the Ghosūṇḍī and Besnagar Inscriptions prove conclusively that the divinity of Kṛishṇa Vāsudeva is not a post-Christian innovation, but is as old at least as the second century B. C. In the Ghosūṇḍī record Saṅkarshaṇa and Vāsudeva are called *Sarveśvara* (lord of all). In the Besnagar inscription of Heliodoros Vāsudeva is called "Devadeva," *i.e.*, the God of gods, and his votary, the ambassador of the Greek king Antialkidas, is called a *Bhāgavata*. In another Besnagar epigraph we have reference to the erection of an excellent temple (*Prāsādottama*) by a *Bhāgavata* during the reign of a king named Bhāgavata. Thus not only the deification of Kṛishṇa, but the existence of the *Bhāgavata* sect preceded the birth of Jesus Christ by at least two centuries. The testimony of the *Mahābhāshya* of Patañjali points to the same conclusion. The identification of Vāsudeva and the god Vishṇu is clearly implied in the *Taittirīya Āraṇyaka*[1] which, according to Dr. Keith, cannot be placed later than the third century B.C. The *Āraṇyaka* was known to Āpastamba who must have lived two or three centuries before Christ.[2]

1 X, I, 6.

2 Bühler's *Introduction to the Sūtras of Āpastamba*, pp. xxv, xliii; *The Cambridge History of India*, Vol. I, p. 249.

As regards the second point, Telang rightly points out that the transition from a great human hero to a hero regarded as an incarnation of the Deity is neither so unusual nor inexplicable that we must imagine some external influence to explain it. What external influence was at work in the apotheosis of Kapila, of Pārśvanātha or of Buddha? Even if we assume, for argument's sake, that there was some external influence, it could not have been the influence of Christianity, because Kṛishṇa was already worshipped as the God of gods two centuries before the birth of Christ.

We now come to the legend of *Śvetadvīpa* which occurs in the *Śāntiparva* of the *Mahābhārata*.[1] Uparichara Vasu performs an *Aśvamedha* sacrifice in which Bṛihaspati is the priest, and Ekata, Dvita, and Trita act as overseers (*Sadasya*). No animals are killed on the occasion, and the oblations are prepared in accordance with the precepts of the *Āraṇyakas*.[2] The *Bhagavat*, the God of gods, being invisible, takes the offering and carries it off without showing Himself to Bṛihaspati. Bṛihaspati is angry, when Ekata, Dvita and Trita explain to him that God is to be seen only by those on whom He shows His Grace. They themselves once went to the White Island (*Śveta dvīpa*) to see Hari or Nārāyaṇa, performed austerities for a long

1 XII, 335-339.

2 Was Sarvatāta of the Ghosuṇḍī Inscription an *Aśvamedhayājin* of this type ?

time, but were told that Nārāyaṇa was not to be seen by them, as they were not His *Bhaktas.* They give an account of the White Island and its inhabitants. We have next an account of Nārada's visit to the Island and his success in seeing Nārāyaṇa. Weber supposes that in this narrative of the three *Ṛishis* Ekata, Dvita and Trita, we have a description of a Christian worship that certain Hindu pilgrims might have witnessed.

Lassen concurs in the belief that some Brāhmaṇas became acquainted with Christianity in some country lying to the north of India, and brought home some Christian doctrines.[1] This he considers to be supported by—

(*a*) the name of the White Island and the colour of its inhabitants, so different from that of the Indians;

(*b*) the ascription to these people of the worship of an Unseen God, while the Indians of the same period had images of their deities ;

(*c*) the attribution to them of faith, the efficacy of which is not an ancient Indian tenet ;

(*d*) the value attributed to prayer, which is a less important element in Indian than in Christian rites ; and

[1] J. Muir, *Metrical Translations fram Sanskrit Writers*, Introduction, pp. xxviii ff.

Lassen, *Indische Alterthumskunde*, 2nd edition, Vol. II, 1118 ff.

(*e*) the fact that the doctrine which they learnt is described as one only made known to the Indians at a late period.

Lassen holds it as the most likely supposition that Parthia was the country where the Brāhmaṇas met with Christian missionaries. Weber prefers Alexandria or Asia Minor. According to Dr. Macnicol it probably refers to some Christian settlement to the north of India. Kennedy says,[1] "The direction can only point to some place beyond the great mountain ranges, to Bactria, perhaps to Lake Issykul." Garbe has identified the Śvetadvīpa with the shores of the Balkhash sea.[2]

Dr. Seal in his *Comparative Studies in Vaishṇavism and Christianity*, observes : "This *Nārāyaṇīya* record, in my opinion, contains decisive evidence of an actual journey or voyage undertaken by some Indian *Vaishṇavas* to the coasts of Egypt or Asia Minor, and makes an attempt in the Indian eclectic fashion to include Christ among the *Āvatārs* or Incarnations of the Supreme Spirit Nārāyaṇa, as Buddha came to be included in a later age."[3] He refers to the following passage of the *Mahābhārāta* :[4]

Chhatrākṛitiśīrshā meghaughaninādāḥ
Samamushkachatushkā rājīvachchhadapādāḥ

1 J. R. A. S., 1907, p. 482.

2 *Indien und das Christentum*, pp. 192 ff.

3 P. 30.

4 *Mbh.*, xii, 335, 11.

Shashṭyā dantairyuktāḥ
śuklairashṭābhirdaṁshṭrābhirye
Jihvābhirye viśvavaktraṁ
lelihyante sūryaprakhyam.

"Their heads seem to be like umbrellas. Their voice is deep like that of looming clouds. Each of them has four *mushkas*, a hundred lotus-feet, sixty white teeth and eight tusks. With their tongues they licked the universal-faced god of sunlike effulgence."

According to Dr. Seal [1] "the Eucharist is here described. The inhabitants drink up the Logos *Sūryaprakhyaṁ viśvavaktraṁ devam.* All these epithets are applicable to the Logos, especially as conceived by the Syrian Christians and Gnostics."

The highly imaginative character of the description of the White Island and its inhabitants, as well as some indications in the narrative that it is not to be taken literally, has however convinced some scholars, that the story is a mere flight of fancy. The *Śvetadvīpa* is said to lie to the north of the Ocean of Milk, and to the north-west of Mount Meru, and above it by 32,000 Yojanas.[2] "I should like to know," asks Telang, "what geography has any notion of the quarter of this earth where we are to look for that sea of milk and mount of gold. Consider next the description

1 Comp. Studies, p. 53.
2 *Mbh.*, xii, 335, 8, 9.

of the wonderful people inhabiting this wonderful *Dvīpa.*

Te Sahasrārchchishaṁ devaṁ
praviśanti sanātanam
Anindriyā nirāhārā
anishpandāḥ sugandhinaḥ.[1]

"They enter that eternal deity of a thousand rays. They have no organs of senses. They do not take any food. Their eyes are winkless and they emit a sweet smell."

"It will be news to the world, that there were in Alexandria or elsewhere a whole people without any organs of sense, who ate nothing, and who entered the Sun—whatever that may mean! Remember, too, that the instruction which Nārada receives in this wonderful land is not received from its inhabitants, but from *Bhagavat,* from God Himself. Nor let it be forgotten, that the doctrines which the Deity there announces to Nārada cannot be shown to have any connexion whatever with Christianity......................the whole of the prelection addressed to Nārada bears on its face its essentially Indian character, in the references to the three qualities, to the twenty-five primal principles, to the description of final emancipation as absorption or entrance into the Divinity, and various other matters of the like character."[2]

[1] XII, 336, 29.

[2] *Introductory Essay to the Bhagavadgītā*, p. xxxv.

We have already pointed out that the distant abode of the "thousand-rayed" *deva* of sun-like effulgence, laved by the sea of milk, has a suspicious likeness with the *parama pada* of Vishṇu with its well of honey where pious men rejoice and, no doubt, sing the praise of the deity "who envelopes the earth on every side with beams of light (*mayukhaiḥ*)." The favoured votaries who have no organs of sense and yet use their tongues do so in the manner of the perfect being of the *Gītā* who is *Sarvendriyaguṇābhāsa, Sarvendriya-vivarjita*.

Even assuming that the story is not a 'flight of fancy,' there are still grave reasons for doubting the correctness of Weber's theory.

"The fact," says Hopkins,[1] "that the 'one god' is already a hackneyed phrase of philosophy; that there is no resemblance to a trinitarian god; that the hymn sung to this one god contains no trace of Christian influence, but is on the other hand thoroughly native in tone and phraseology, being as follows: 'Victory to thee thou god with lotus eyes; Reverence to thee, thou creator of all things; Reverence be to thee, O Vishṇu (Hṛishīkeça); thou Great Person; first born one;' all these facts indicate that if the White Islanders are indeed to be regarded as foreigners worshipping a strange god, that god is strictly monotheis-

1 *The Religions of India*, p. 432.

tic and not trinitarian. Weber lays stress on the expression 'first-born,' which he thinks refers to Christ; but the epithet is old (Vedic), and is common, and means no more than 'primal deity.'"

The name of the White Island and the colour of its inhabitants ("*śvetāḥ Pumāṁsaḥ*") do not necessarily prove that some Christian settlement (Parthia) is meant. Hopkins observes [1] that the white men of the White Island 'in the north-west' may be Kashmere Brāhmaṇas. The question whether Lassen or Hopkins is right cannot be definitely settled. There seems no more reason to reject Hopkins' theory than to accept the theory of Lassen.

As regards the second point of Lassen we need only point out that the God of the White Islanders was invisible only to those who were not his Bhaktas—*na sa śakyastvabhaktena drashṭuṁ devaḥ kathañchana* [2]—but could be seen by His *Bhaktas*. He was therefore not altogether an Unseen God. Moreover it has not been proved that all the Indians of the period when the *Nārāyaṇīya* was composed had images of their deities. The most advanced philosophers and the *Ṛishis* who meditated upon God in the woods usually dispensed with images. The 'worship of an unseen God'

1 *The Great Epic of India*, p. 116.
2 Mbh., xii, 336-54.

was familiar to the Indians from the age of the *Ṛig Veda*.[1]

Lassen opines that the efficiency of 'faith' is not an ancient Indian tenet. This is hardly correct. Dr. Seal observes : [2] "The Vedic Hymns are replete with sentiments of piety and reverence (*Bhakti* and *Śraddhā*) in the worship of the gods......The *Upāsanā Kāṇḍas* of the *Āraṇyakas* and *Upanishads* lay the foundations of the *Bhakti-Mārga*, way of Devotion or Faith."[3] The *Pātañjala Yoga Sūtras* lay down devout worship of the Lord as the surest and swiftest means of attaining *Yoga* as a means to Emancipation. Sir R. G. Bhandarkar also proves that *Bhakti* had a purely Indian origin.[4] "The thought of India," says Dr. Keith,[5] "started from a religion which had in Varuṇa a god of decidedly moral character and the simple worship of that deity with its consciousness of sin and trust in the divine forgiveness is doubtless one of the first roots of Bhakti" (loving faith). "There is much," says Dr. Macnicol,[6] "in the prayers and hymns to Varuṇa that brings back to one who knows it the lofty language of Hebrew seers and psalmists."

1 *Cf.* the hymns to Hiraṇyagarbha.

2 *Comparative Studies in Vaishnavism and Christianity*, p. 5.

3 p. 8.

4 Vaiṣṇavism, pp. 28-29.

5 J.R.A.S., 1915, p. 834.

6 Indian Theism, pp. 11 f.

Prof. Garbe, in his translation of the *Bhagavad-gītā*,[1] observes that a monotheistic religion, in which the object of worship was looked upon as a kindly, not a terrible, deity, would naturally beget the feelings of *Bhakti* in the hearts of his worshippers. Pāṇini actually speaks of *Bhakti* dedicated to Vāsudeva. Edmund Hardy points out that the word *bhatti* (*bhakti*) is to be found in the sense of "love," "self-resignation" in the *Jātakas*, while in the *Theragāthā* it passes into the specific sense of "devotion to God."[2]

The statement of Lassen that prayer is less important an element in Indian than in Christian rites is also not accurate. From the age of the *Ṛig Veda* to that of the latest *Purāṇas* prayer formed an important part of Hindu worship. "There is in fact," says Professor Macdonell,[3] "no hymn to Varuṇa and the Ādityas in which the prayer for forgiveness does not occur, as in the hymns to other deities the prayer for worldly goods."

> How e'er we who thy people are,
> O Varuṇa, thou shining god,
> Thy *ṛita* injure day by day,
> Yet give us over nor to death,
> Nor to the blow of angry foe.[4]

[1] pp. 29 ff.

[2] Garbe's *Introduction to the Bhagavadgītā*, translated by Utgikar, pp. 16-17.

[3] Macdonell's *Vedic Mythology*, p. 27.

[4] R. V., i, 25, 1, 2 (Hopkins' translation).

It is clear from what we have said that the doctrines which the travellers to the *Śvetadvīpa* learnt were not imported to India at a late period.

As regards the *Nārāyaṇīya* verse[1] referred to by Dr. Seal, the following translation is given by Pratāpchandra Rāy, C.I.E. :[2]

"Their heads seem to be like umbrellas. Their voices are deep like that of the clouds. Each of them has four *mushkas*. The soles of their feet were marked by hundreds of lines. They had sixty teeth all of which were white (and large) and eight smaller ones. They had many tongues. With those tongues they seemed to lick the very sun whose face is turned towards every direction."

Where are we to find the men with four *mushkas*, and sixty teeth? The whole description seems to be a flight of imagination—an attempt on the part of "mythologizing philosophers" to depict an Isle of the Blessed where perfect beings of *Bhāgavata* fancy hold communion with their beloved Lord. The omission of the name of the Buddha from the list of the *Avatāras* given in the *Nārāyaṇīya*[3] shows that the author was singularly wanting in that spirit of eclecticism, which, according to Dr. Seal, led him to include Christ among the *Avatāras* of Nārāyaṇa.

[1] Mbh., xii, 335, 11.
[2] Çāntiparva, Vol. II, pp. 744-45.
[3] Mbh., xii, 339, 103-04.

We have now to consider whether there is any reliable evidence of Christian influence on the legends of the Child Kṛishṇa and on the celebration of his birth-day.

Weber observes:[1] "The most difficult point in connection with the festival of the birth-day of Kṛishṇa lies clearly in the description, and particularly in the pictorial representation, of him as a suckling at his mother's breast, and in the homage paid to the mother, represented as lying on a couch in a cow-house, who has borne him, 'the lord of the world,' in her womb. Such a representation of the god is a strange contrast to the other representations of him—to that of the epos, for example, in which he appears as a warrior-hero and is moreover, the only thing of its kind in India."

According to the great German scholar, the birth-day festival of Kṛishṇa, and the pictorial representation of him as a suckling at his mother's breast, which forms an integral part of that festival, are borrowed from the legends regarding the virgin and the representations of the *Madonna lactans*, and came to India from the West at a time when "The Madonna and the child" had already on their side won a firm and sure place in the Christian ritual.

[1] Ind. Ant., 1874, p. 21.

Weber adds that "in the train of the birth-day festival we must suppose that other legendary matters came to India which are found in the accounts of the *Harivaṁśa*, of the *Jaimini Bhārata*, and in some interpolated passages of the *Mahābhārata*, in the *Purāṇas*, specially in the *Bhāgavata Purāṇa* and its offshoots which describe and embellish the birth and childhood of Kṛishṇa with notices which remind us irresistibly of Christian legends. Take, for example, the statement of the *Vishṇu Purāṇa* that Nanda, the foster-father of Kṛishṇa, at the time of the latter's birth, went with his pregnant wife Yaśodā to Mathurā to pay taxes (*cf.* Luke II, 4, 5) or the pictorial representation of the birth of Kṛishṇa in the cowstall or shepherd's hut, that corresponds to the manger, and of the shepherds, shepherdesses, the ox and the ass that stand round the woman as she sleeps peacefully on her couch without fear of danger. Then the stories of the persecutions of Kaṁsa, of the massacre of the innocents, of the passage across the river (Christophoros), of the wonderful deeds of the child, of the healing-virtue of the water in which he was washed, etc., etc. Whether the accounts given in the *Jaimini Bhārata* of the raising to life by Kṛishṇa of the dead son of Duḥśalā, of the cure of *Kubjā*, of her pouring a vessel of ointment over him, of the power of his look to take away sin, and other subjects of the kind came to India in the same connection with the birth-day festival may remain an open question."

Weber does not stand alone in his view concerning the influence of Christianity on the legends of Kṛishṇa. "The coincidences," says Hopkins,[1] "as some scholars marvellously regard them, between the legends of Christ and Kṛishṇa are too extraordinary to be accepted as such. They are direct importations, not accidental coincidences .... It remains only to ask from which side is the borrowing ? Considering how late are these Kṛishṇa legends in India there can be no doubt that the Hindu borrowed the tales, but not the name; for the last assumption is quite improbable because Kṛishṇa (=Christ ?) is native enough, and Jishṇu is as old as the *Rig Veda*."

"About the first century of the Christian era," says Sir R. G. Bhandarkar,[2] "the boygod of a wandering tribe of Ābhiras came to be identified with Vāsudeva. In the course of their wanderings eastward from Syria or Asia Minor they brought with them, probably, traditions of the birth of Christ in a stable, the massacre of the innocents, etc., and the name Christ itself. The name became recognised as Kṛishṇa, as this word is often pronounced by some Indians as Krista or Kusta. And thus the traditional legends brought

1 *The Religions of India*, p. 430.

2 Ind. Ant., 1912, p. 15.

by the Ābhīras became engrafted on the story of Vāsudeva Kṛishṇa of India."

Dr. Macnicol is inclined to believe that about the middle of the seventh century A. D. Nestorian missions (which are believed to have entered India from the north in the year 639) may have brought stories of the child Christ as well as pictures and ritual observances which affected the story of Kṛishṇa as related in the *Purāṇas*, and the worship of Kṛishṇa especially in relation to the celebration of his birth festival. To this belong the birth in a cow-house among cattle, the massacre of the innocents, the story that his foster-father Nanda was travelling at the time to Mathurā to pay tax or tribute to Kaṁsa, and other details to be found in the various *Purāṇas* and in the *Jaimini Bhārata*.

No one can help being struck by the points of resemblance between the story of the child Kṛishṇa and that of the child Christ. When one investigates, however, one finds that the hypothesis of a plagiarism rests on a weak basis.

With regard to the birth-day festival of Kṛishṇa, the representation of him as a suckling at his mother's breast, and the homage paid to the mother, Weber himself points out that the festival of the *Rāmanavamî* presents many striking analogies to the *Kṛishṇa-janmāshṭamî*. The *Rāmāyaṇa*, which is a pre-Christian work according to Prof. Macdonell[1] gives a detailed account of Rāma's birth, and in one passage of that epic Rāma is represented as "resting in the lap of his mother," *māturaṅkagataḥ*.[2] Kennedy observes :[3] "There is no Christian representation of the suckling mother before the twelfth century, but there is a much earlier Hindu one. At Elūra we have a bas relief of the seven divine mothers each with her child on her knee or beside her ; and Varāhî, the third of the seven, is giving suck to her infant." According to Piper's representation, the adoration of Virgin Mary was even in the fourth century A. D. far from prominent, and we are to date its decisive introduction from the Nestorian disputes in the fifth century.[4] If the decisive introduction of the worship of the Virgin dated from the fifth century, its propagation in distant foreign lands must have taken place in a later age. But the association of Kṛishṇa with Devakī, his mother, is, as is well known, as old as the *Chhāndogya Upanishad*. We learn from the Bhitarî Pillar Inscription that early in the fifth century A.D. Devakī already occupied a prominent place in the Kṛishṇa cultus. In his *History of Fine Art in India and Ceylon*,[5] V. Smith mentions

1 Sanskrit Literature, pp. 307-310.

2 Ind. Ant., 1874, p. 21, n.

3 J. R. A. S., 1907, p. 484.

4 Ind. Ant., 1874, p. 47.

5 p. 164.

"a composition, nearly life-size, at Pathārî in the Bhopāl Agency, believed to represent the new-born Kṛishṇa lying by the side of his mother, who is watched by five attendants." The composition belongs to the Gupta Age. Bas reliefs of Badami dating from the early Chalukya period depict several scenes connected with the child Kṛishṇa and in one of these we find two females standing each with a child in her arms. Mr. R. D. Banerji thinks that these females represent Yaśodā and Rohiṇī with Kṛishṇa and Balarāma in their laps.[1] The *Bhāgavatas* did not borrow the idea of a mother-goddess from the Christians. Dr. Keith observes :[2] "Rhys Davids has brought evidence to show that there was in early days a widespread worship of Śrī comparable to the worship of Here or Athene in many Greek cities which with the rise of Christianity became transmuted into the adoration of the Madonna." The worship of Śrī is as old as the *Śatapatha Brāhmaṇa*[3] and the *Bodhāyana Dharma Sūtra*.[4] We have representations of this goddess at Bharhut and other ancient Buddhist centres[5] and also on the coins of Rājuvula.[6] In a letter to the author Grierson suggests that the homage

1 *Memoirs of the Archaeological Survey of India*, No. 25, p. 25.

2 J.R.A.S., 1907, p. 491.

3 ix, 4, 3.

4 ii, 5-24.

5 *Buddhist India*, pp. 217-218.

6 Cunningham's *Coins of Ancient India*, p. 86.

paid to the suckling mother is a relic of the Buddhist worship of Hāritī, the "Buddhist Madonna."[1] Recent discoveries at Mahenjo-Daro in Sind prove that the worship of the Mother Goddess can claim a hoary antiquity.[2]

As regards the pastoral associations of Kṛishṇa we have already pointed out that Vishṇu, the Vedic deity with whom Kṛishṇa is identified in the pre-Christian *Taittirîya Āraṇyaka*, is called, in the *Ṛig Veda*, *Gopā* which means "protector of cows" according to Macdonell and Keith,[3] and "herdsman" according to Hopkins.[4] In the *Ṛig Veda*, I. 155.6 Vishṇu is called "ever young" *Yuvā akumāraḥ*. The epithets *Gopā* and *Yuvā akumāraḥ* of the Vedic Vishṇu might have been suggestive of the *Purāṇic* tale of the youthful herdsman of Vṛindāvana, just as the three strides of the same god suggested the legend of the Dwarf *Avatāra*.

Mr. Jayaswāl points out[5] that before the *Baudhāyana Dharma Sūtras* Dāmodara and Govinda were known deities. This disposes of the view that the Kṛishṇa worship in the child and pastoral form owes its origin to Christianity.

1 *Cf.* Foucher, *The Beginnings of Buddhist Art*, translated by Thomas, pp. 171 ff.

2 Sir John Marshall, *Mahenjo-Daro and the Indus Civilisation*, I, Ch. V.

3 *The Vedic Index*, Vol. I, p. 238.

4 The Religions of India, p. 57.

5 Ind. Ant., 1918, p. 84.

It has been observed by Sir Charles Eliot[1] that the first allusions to the presence of Christians in Parthia, Bactria and the borderlands of India date from the third century and that the oldest account of Christian communities in Southern India is the narrative of Cosmas Indicopleustes (*c.* 525 A.D.). Now, the worship of the pastoral Kṛishṇa-Vishṇu in the early centuries of the Christian era in Southern India is clearly suggested by a significant royal name, "Vishṇu gopa," occurring in the Allahabad Pillar Inscription of the middle of the fourth century A.D. A Junāgaḍh record of A.D. 457-58 refers to a provincial administrator as one "whose life is devoted to the feet of Govinda" (*Govindapādārpitajīvita*).

The enmity between Kaṁsa and Kṛishṇa is referred to as familiar in Patañjali's *Mahābhāshya* (usually assigned to the second century B.C.), and it is fair to conclude, as Macnicol does, that the legend of the attempt of Kaṁsa to kill Kṛishṇa in his childhood was also extant at that period.

The story of the passage across the river need not be traced to a Christian source. In the Vinaya Texts,[2] we have the story of Buddha's miraculous crossing of the Ganges.

The *Harivaṁśa* and the *Purāṇas* in which the stories about the child Kṛishṇa, referred to by Weber, Hopkins and others, occur, are really not

1 *Hinduism and Buddhism*, Vol. III, 414.

2 Part II, p. 104.

so late works as these scholars would have us believe. The *Harivaṁśa* and all the eighteen *Purāṇas* are mentioned in the *Mahābhārata* and we know from the Khoh Inscription of Śarvanātha that the Great Epic was complete, that is to say, it contained one hundred thousand *Ślokas*, in the sixth century A.D. We have independent proof of the celebrity of the *Vāyu*, *Āgni*, *Bhāgavata*, *Mārkaṇḍeya* and *Skanda Purāṇas* in the seventh century A.D.[1] The *Harivaṁśa* is mentioned as a famous work by Subandhu, a writer of the seventh century A.D.[2] A *Bhavishyat Purāṇa* is mentioned in the *Dharma Sūtra* of Āpastamba.[3]

There is reason to believe that the *Vāyu*, *Brahmāṇḍa* and the *Vishṇu Purāṇas* were compiled during the reign of Chandragupta I, the founder of the Gupta dynasty, who is said to have ruled from 320 A.D. to about 335 A.D. "It seems to be to his reign that the verses in the *Purāṇas* defining the Gupta dominions refer."[4] Mr. Pargiter, in his valuable work, the *Dynastics of the Kali Age*, adduces good grounds for placing the original *Matsya Purāṇa* in the third century A.D. Some of the Christian Scriptures from which the *Purāṇas* are alleged to have borrowed the stories about the

1 See V. Smith's Early History of India, 3rd edition, p. 22.

2 Weber's Ind. Lit., p. 119.

3 Bühler's Introduction, p. xxviii.

4 Allan's *Catalogue of the Coins of the Gupta Dynasties*, p. xix.

child Kṛishṇa are not much older.[1] Jackson[2] refers to the discovery at Mandor in Mārwār of sculptures of certain exploits of the child Kṛishṇa which are of very early date.[3] Sten Konow finds a reference to the youthful deeds of Kṛishṇa (Siri-Kaḍāra) in the Hāthigumphā Inscription of Khāravela.[4] Echoes of some of the Kṛishṇaite legends are found in Jaina Sculptures in Mathurā belonging to the first century B.C.[5] We have already seen that many of the Purāṇic stories about the child Kṛishṇa are illustrated by bas reliefs at Badami dating from the sixth century A.D. Tales about Kṛishṇa's sports on the banks of the Jumna travelled to the most distant countries of Indo-China in the ninth century A.D.[6]

We now come to the theory of Sir R. G. Bhandarkar. We learn from the *Periplus of the Erythraean Sea* that the Ābhīras were already settled in Western India ("Abiria"), in the first century A.D. They are also mentioned by Patañjali.[7] How could they bring with them traditions of the birth of Christ in a stable, of the

1 Telang's *Introductory Essay to the Bhagavadgītā*, pp. xxiv, lxii, lxiii, n.

2 J.R.A.S., 1908, p. 533.

3 See *Arch. Survey Report, W. India*, 1906-7, p. 33, para. 24.

4 *Acta Orientalia*, I, 1923, 39.

5 Winternitz, A History of Indian Literature—English translation, Vol. II, 463n.

6 Eliot, *Hinduism and Buddhism*, II, 159n.

7 Ind. Ant. 1918, p. 36.

massacre of the innocents and so on? Mr. V. Kanakasabhai, in his *Tamils Eighteen Hundred Years Ago*,[1] says that the Ayar (Ābhīras) had a tradition that they came into the Tamil land, along with the founder of the Pāṇḍyan family, *i.e.*, several centuries before Christ. Their name Ayar is derived from the Dravidian "Ā" meaning a cow.

Referring to Macnicol's conjecture that Nestorian Missions may have brought stories of the child Christ about the middle of the seventh century A.D., Dr. Keith observes that it is not true that Nestorian Missionaries entered the north of India in 639 A.D.[2] This error is borrowed from Garbe and ultimately from Sir G. Grierson,[3] but for giving it wide currency the latter has already made complete amends by his correction of Takakusu on whom the ultimate responsibility for the mistake rests.[4]

Weber and his followers do not seek to present Kṛishṇaism as a distorted form of Christianity. They do not mean to assert that in Kṛishṇa India ever paid divine honour to Jesus. The Hindu god, in their opinion, "had only arrogated to himself a certain number of

1 p. 57.

2 J.R.A.S., 1915, pp. 839-840.

3 See his article *Bhakti Mārga* in Hastings' *Encyclopaedia of Religion and Ethics*, ii, 548.

4 J.R.A.S., 1913, 144.

Christian endowments." But Dr. Lorinser, in his *Bhagavadgītā*, goes further than this. He arrives at the singular conclusion that the author of the Hindu poem knew and used the Gospels and the Christian Fathers. His arguments may be summarised as follows.[1]

Saṅkarāchārya lived in the eighth century A.D. ; from that it is to be inferred that the Gītā was composed some five centuries earlier, *i.e.*, in the third century A.D. ; at that time there were Christian communities in India ; and there was also an Indian translation of the New Testament of which we have positive proof in the writings of St. Chrysostom. " In this way," Dr. Lorinser goes on to observe, " the possibility that the composer of the *Bhagavadgītā* may have been acquainted not merely with the general teaching of Christianity, but also with the very writings of the New Testament, might be shown in a very natural way, without the necessity of having recourse to rash hypothesis." The Doctor finds in the *Gītā* passages, and these not single and obscure, but numerous and clear, which present a surprising similarity to passages in the New Testament, and concludes that the composer was acquainted with the writings of the New Testament and used them as he thought fit. He places side by side the most important of these passages in the *Gītā*, and the corresponding texts of the New Testament.

[1] See *Indian Antiquary*, Vol. II, 283 *et seq.*

Dr. Lorinser further observes that the ideas *Śraddhā* and *Bhakti* are not originally Indian, but that they have been taken over from Christianity. In his opinion the incarnation of Vishṇu as Kṛishṇa—the only one represented as a truly human incarnation of the person of the god—is an imitation of the Christian dogma regarding the person of Christ.

Let us examine the arguments of Dr. Lorinser. It is not difficult to prove that the *Gītā* is much older than the third century A.D. While discussing the age of the *Mahābhārata*, Hopkins observes :—[1] "We may say with comparative certainty that, with the exception of the parts latest added, the introduction to the first book and the last book, even the pseudo-epic was completed as early as 200 A.D." By pseudo-epic Hopkins means the didactic books, notably the *Śānti* and the *Anuśāsana Parvas.*[2] As the *Bhagavadgītā* is referred to in the *Śāntiparva* it must be assigned to a period considerably anterior to the second century A.D. Hopkins says explicitly[3] that the *Gītā* is "unquestionably one of the older poems in the epic." He further observes[4] that "the *Gītā* and the Gambling scene are, as wholes, metrically and stylistically more antique than are

1 *The Great Epic of India*, p. 387.
2 The G.E.I., p. 381.
3 p. 205.
4 p. 402.

the Anugītā and the extravaganzas in the battle-books." In his *Ethics of India*[1] Hopkins admits the validity of the present author's contention that the triple formula *dama, tyāga* and *apramāda*, occurring in the didactic epic, is quoted by the *Bhāgavata* Inscription of Heliodoros belonging to the second century B.C.

Regarding the coincidences between passages in the *Gītā* and in the New Testament, Dr. Macnicol says[2] that a careful examination of the parallels that have been traced shows the resemblances to be in many cases purely verbal and unreal, while others can be paralleled from the *Upanishads* which are certainly pre-Christian. When Kṛishṇa says "of creations I am the beginning and the end.........of letters I am the Syllable A"[3] the likeness to the words in *Revelation* (i, 8), "I am Alpha and Omega, the beginning and the ending, which is, and which was, and which is to come," is no doubt striking, but Kṛishṇa is only repeating what is found in the *Upanishads*, "Brahma is the A."[4] "Kṛishṇa's identification of himself with everything in the Universe is in full agreement with the claims for Brahman in the *Upanishads*, and that among the lists of those things, that he is there, should be found some of

1 p. 171n.
2 *Indian Theism*, p. 276.
3 *Gītā*, x, 20-33.
4 Hopkins, The Religions of India, p. 226.

the names such as the truth, the light, the way, which are applied to Christ, and especially to Christ in His aspect as the Eternal Word, is not surprising and cannot be said to prove indebtedness."[1] Referring to the striking similarity between the declaration of the *Gītā*, ix, 29, "They who devoutly worship me are in me, and I in them," and John, vi, 56, "He that eateth my flesh, and drinketh my blood dwelleth in me, and I in him," Dr. Muir observes[2] that "the condition of oneness with the speaker is different in each case" and that it is that oneness with him only that is common to the two texts." In the *Ṛig Veda* some passages occur which in part convey the same or a similar idea. Thus in ii, 11, 12, it is said: "O Indra, we sages have been in thee;" and in x, 142, 1, "This worshipper, O Agni, hath been in thee: O Son of strength, he has no other kinship; in viii, 92, 32, the worshippers say to Indra, "thou art ours, and we thine—*tvamasmākaṁ tavasmasi.*"

Let us take a few more parallel passages.

"He is far from darkness,"

"*Sarvasya dhātāramachintyarūpam*
Ādityavarṇaṁ tamasaḥ parastāt.[3]

[1] *Indian Theism*, p. 276.
[2] Ind. Ant., 1875, pp. 79-80.
[3] Gītā, viii, 9.

"Light of lights, far from darkness is his name."

"*jyotishāmapi tajjyotistamasaḥ paramuchyate.*[1]

"God is light, and in him is no darkness at all."[2]

The words here translated "far from darkness" (*tamasaḥ parastāt*) are not peculiar to the *Gītā*, but occur also in the *Muṇḍaka Upanishad.*[3] The word *tamasaspari* meaning "above, or beyond the darkness" occurs also in the *Ṛig Veda.*[4] "Gazing towards the upper light beyond the darkness, we have ascended to the highest luminary Sūrya, a God among the gods." Curiously enough this was one of the verses which Kṛishṇa learnt from Ghora Āṅgirasa.[5] In the *Gītā* the words *tamasaḥ parastāt* are immediately preceded by '*āditya-varṇam*' "the sun-coloured." The *Gītākāra* had thus no need to borrow anything from the Bible. Dr. Muir observes "most of the verses cited from that poem (the *Gītā*) by Dr. Lorinser as parallel to texts in the Bible appear to me either to exhibit no very close resemblance to the latter, or to be such as might naturally have occurred to the Indian writer, and to offer therefore only an accidental similarity."[6]

1 Gītā, xiii, 17.
2 I John, i, 5.
3 II, ii, 6.
4 I, 50, 10.
5 Chh., iii, 17, 7.
6 Ind. Ant., 1875, p. 81.

Dr. Lorinser finds that it is the Gospel of John in particular from which the composer of the Gītā has taken the most important phrases. We have pointed out that the *Gītā* existed long before the second century A.D., while the Gospel of John, according to Dr. Strauss, 'was not known until after the middle of the second century A.D.'[1] Strauss adds that the Fourth Gospel "bears every indication of having arisen upon a foreign soil, and under the influence of a philosophy of the time unknown to the original circle in which Jesus lived." Foreign influence on early Christianity is seen by some scholars in the nimbus round the head of the Saviour and a plurality of hands assigned to the Madonna.[2]

We now come to the doctrines of *Śraddhā*, *Bhakti* and *Avatāra*. Telang observes :[3] "In the comment on Pāṇini, ii, 2, 34 occur the following examples : *Śraddhāmedhe* and *Śraddhātapaso*. Now, when we observe that these examples are given to illustrate the rule that in copulative compounds the more important term stands before the less important, it becomes clear that *Śraddhā* was in the time of Patañjali regarded as a more important element in a religious life than even *medhā* and *tapas*. The *Chhāndogya Upanishad* is one of the oldest of the Upanishads, and in it we have the

[1] Telang's *Introductory Essay*, p. lxii.

[2] *Ind. Ant.*, 1874, pp. 50-52.

[3] *Introductory Essay to the Bhagavad-Gītā*, pp. lxxxi-lxxxii.

passage *yadeva vidyayā karoti Śraddhayopanishadā tadeva vīryavattaraṁ bhavati*, where we see the value ascribed to *Śraddhā*, faith mingled with reverence.[1]

It has already been shown that the ideas that *Bhakti* connotes are found in the Varuṇa and Āditya hymns of the *Ṛig Veda*, and that the word in its religious application is pre-Christian.[2] *Parā bhakti*, supreme devotion to God, is taught in the *Śvetāśvatara Upanishad* and *bhakti* in the sense of religious adoration is clearly implied in the Buddhist *Theragāthā*.[3]

The incarnation, *Avatāra*, of Vishṇu as Kṛishṇa is not a post-Christian innovation. It is clearly implied in the *Taittirīya Āraṇyaka*[4] which is certainly a pre-Christian work.[5] The book is referred to by Āpastamba. The germ of the theory of *Avatāra*, Descent or Incarnation, already appears in the *Brāhmaṇa* literature. In the *Śatapatha Brāhmaṇa*[6] we find the statement that "having assumed the form of a tortoise Prajāpati created offspring"; and again that "in the form of a boar he raised the earth from the bottom of the ocean."[7] The *Brāhmaṇas* also state that Vishṇu assumed the

1 Chh. Up., i, 1, 10. *Cf.* also Chhāndogya, vii, 19—*Śraddhāṁ Bhagavo vijijñāsa iti.*

Cf. Pāṇini, iv, 3, 95; iv, 3, 98.

3 V. 370, Garbe, Introduction to the *Bhagavad-Gītā*, trans. by Utgikar, pp. 14-17.

4 X, 1, 6. 5 J.R.A.S., 1915, p. 840. 6 7, 5, 1, 5; 14, 1, 2, 11.

7 See *Vedic Mythology*, p. 41 *et seq.*

form of a dwarf in order by artifice to recover the earth for the gods from the Asuras by taking his three strides.

Barth says:[1] "The theory of the *Avatāras* appears to us to be a purely Indian one.........We have indicated elsewhere the analogy that exists between it and the theory of the successive apparitions of Buddha, and this last appears to have been conceived prior to our era, since we find it figuring in the bas-reliefs of Barahat."

We find what is difficult to distinguish from the theory of *Avatāra* in the *Saddharmapuṇḍarīka*,[2] a Buddhist work, which was probably composed before any Christian missionaries came to India since it obtained great celebrity in the opening centuries of the Christian era, and was translated into Chinese in the third century A.D. The story of St. Thomas' visit to India in the first century A.D. is, according to V. Smith,[3] "pure mythology." The existence of the Christian Church of South India may be traced back only to the third century, but not earlier.[4] Eliot observes that the oldest account of Christian communities in Southern India is the narrative of Cosmas Indicopleustes (*c.* 525 A.D.).[5]

1 The *Religions of India*, p. 222.

2 xv, 7-9, Kern's translation, p. 308.

3 E. H. I⁴., p. 248.

4 E. H. I., p. 250.

5 *Hinduism and Buddhism*, III, 414; *cf.* Carpenter, *Theism in Mediaeval India*, 522.

LECTURE IV

Bhāgavatism in the Scythian, Gupta and Post-Gupta Periods

The history of the *Bhāgavata* religion from the first to the third century A.D. is, at present, in a state of utmost confusion and darkness. There are some Buddhist works of the period, *e.g.*, the *Buddha-charita*, and the *Mahāyāna Śraddhotpāda* (Awakening of Faith) attributed to Aśvaghosha, which, in our opinion, show some acquaintance with Bhāgavatism, but they do not to any great extent illumine the darkness. The difficulty of finding any Brāhmaṇical works, which may with certainty be referred to this period, excludes them from the domain of the historian.

Kṛishṇa appears to be mentioned in four famous inscriptions of the period, namely, the Mora stone slab inscription of the time of the Mahākshatrapa Rājuvula,[1] the Mathurā Inscription of the time of his son, the Mahākshatrapa Soḍāsa, edited by Mr. R. P. Chanda,[2] the Nāsik Buddhist Cave Inscription of the time of Rājan Vāsiṭhiputa Siri-Pulumāyi[3] and the China Stone Inscription

1 J.R.A.S., 1911, 151.

2 *Memoirs of the Archæological Survey of India*, No. 5.

3 Lüders, Inscription No. 1123.

of the time of Rājan Gotamiputa Siri-Yaña Sātakaṇi.[1] The Mora record seems to contain a reference to images of the *Bhagavat* Vṛishṇi and the five Vīras (heroes), *i.e.*, of Kṛishṇa and the five Pāṇḍava brothers. The Mathurā Inscription, edited by Mr. Ramāprasād Chanda, records the erection of a *toraṇa* (gateway), *vedikā* (terrace) and *chatuḥśāla* (quadrangle) at the *mahāsthāna* (great place) of Bhagavat Vāsudeva, in the reign of the Mahākshatrapa Śoḍāsa. In the Nāsik inscription the name of Kṛishṇa (Keśava) occurs in the following passage: *Ekadhanudharasa ekasurasa ekaBamhaṇasa Rāma-Keśav-Ārjuna-Bhīmasenatulaparakamasa,* "the unique archer, the unique hero, the unique Brāhmaṇa, in prowess equal to Rāma, Keśava, Arjuna and Bhīmasena."[2] This inscription comes from the same province of India to which the Nānāghāṭ record belongs. But it is worthy of note that the characteristic *Bhāgavata* names Saṅkarshaṇa and Vāsudeva are not mentioned, and are substituted by Rāma and Keśava; and the two are not called *Bhagavat*, but only men of prowess. This is exactly what we might expect from a record in a Buddhist cave. It will be remembered that in the Buddhist *Ghata Jātaka* also Vāsudeva and Baladeva figure only as princes and warriors. The China Inscription was published by Bühler as early as

1 Lüders, Inscription No. 1340.

2 *Epigraphia Indica*, Vol. VIII, p. 60.

1889.[1] Mr. N. G. Majumdar is the first to point out that it opens with an invocation of *Bhagavat* Vāsudeva.

Sir John Marshall found at Tumain in Central India an original Vaishṇava temple now dedicated to the goddess Vindhyavāsinī, a form of Durgā. The original building was adorned with vigorous and beautiful carvings representing incidents in the life of Kṛishṇa. Another notable monument was recognised to be a figure of Balarāma assignable to the second or third century A.D.[2]

Mathurā, the birth-place of Bhāgavatism, where the religion was found flourishing by Megasthenes, had ceased to be the stronghold of the faith during the Śaka-Kushān Period. Only two *Bhāgavata* Inscriptions have yet been discovered at the place, or in its immediate neighbourhood, which can be referred with certainty to the period of Scythian rule. The evidence of epigraphy points to the predominance of the Jaina faith, although Buddhism and Serpent worship also appear to have flourished. No less than eighty-seven inscriptions belong to the Jaina faith. The number of Buddhist inscriptions is about fifty-six. The following epigraphs belong to Serpent worship :—

1 Ep. Ind., Vol. I, p. 95 f.

2 Annual Report of the Director General of Archæology in India, 1918-19, p. 21.

(1) Lüders, Inscription No. 63 which records the dedication of a pillar by Devila, the servant or priest at the temple of Dadhikarṇa.

(2) Lüders, Inscription No. 85 which records the dedication of a stone slab in the temple of the divine lord of serpents (*bhagavat nāgendra*) Dadhikarṇa by the sons of the actors of Mathurā, who are praised as the Chāndaka brothers, chief among whom was Nandibala.

(3) Lüders, Inscription No. 52*a*—The Mathurā Nāga Statuette Inscription.

The evidence of serpent worship in Mathurā is important in view of the close association of Kṛishṇa-Vishṇu, called Anantasvāmin in a Gupta record, with Ananta the lord of snakes, the identification of his elder brother, Balarāma, with the serpent king, and the story of Kālīya *nāga* and his suppression by Kṛishṇa recorded in the Purāṇas compiled during the Gupta Period.

The paucity of *Bhāgavata* inscriptions at Mathurā probably indicates that Bhāgavatism did not find much favour at the royal court. The Śaka and Kushān sovereigns who reigned from the first century B.C. to the third century A.D. were usually Śiva worshippers or Buddhists and were, with a few exceptions, probably not well disposed towards the religion of Vāsudeva. The word *Rudra* figures more frequently in royal nomenclature than the name *Vāsudeva*. And the epic bards devoted to *Pītavāsa Janārdana*, the yellow-robed Kṛishṇa, speak with horror of the depredations of Śakas and allied barbarians in the evil age "to come."[1] This anti-*Bhāgavata* attitude was probably one of the causes which brought the foreign kings into conflict with Vaishṇava monarchs like Chandra of the Meharaulî Inscription and the Chandra Guptas of the Gupta dynasty.

No inscription has yet been discovered which throws much light on the state of Bhāgavatism in Northern India during the period which elapsed from the time of Śoḍāsa to the Age of the Guptas. When the veil of darkness is lifted again in the Gupta Period we find the religion flourishing in the Pañjāb, Rājputāna, Central and Western India and Magadha.

The Tuśām Rock Inscription, discovered in the Hissar District of the Pañjāb, which may be assigned to the fourth century A.D. on palæographical grounds, contains an adoration of Vishṇu, "the mighty bee on the water-lily which is the face of Jāmbavatī," and mentions two reservoirs intended for the use of the *Bhagavat*, which are the work of Somatrāta, the great-grandson of *Āryya-Sātvata-Yogāchāryya-Bhagavadbhakta* Yaśastrāta. The nomenclature of this family of Sātvata devotees reminds us of Sarvat(r)āta of the Ghosūṇḍî record and the epithets applied to Yaśastāta prove the Aryan origin of the Sātvata religion

1 Mbh., III, 188.

and point to the close connection between Yoga and Bhakti dedicated to the *Bhagavat* of the Sātvatas, which is one of the most noticeable features of the *Gītā*.

In the Śuśuniā Inscription of Chandravarman that monarch is described as the lord (*adhipati*) of Pushkaraṇa and as a servant (*dāsa*) of *Chakrasvāmin* (wielder of the discus, *i.e.*, Kṛishṇa-Vishṇu). Mahāmahopādhyāya Haraprasād Śāstrī believes, perhaps wrongly, that this king (*Mahārāja*) is identical with the supreme sovereign (*bhūmipati prāpta aikādhirājya*) Chandra of the Meharaulî Iron Pillar Inscription "who in battle in the *Vaṅga* countries turned back with his breast the enemies who uniting together came against him, and by whom having crossed in warfare the seven mouths of the Indus the *Vāhlikas* were conquered." King Chandra set up a lofty standard (*dhvaja*) of *Bhagavat* Vishṇu on the hill called *Vishṇupada* which is probably identical with that part of the Delhi Ridge on which the column stands.

An inscription of the time of Naravarman, regarded by some scholars, without adequate reason, as the younger brother of Chandravarman, has been discovered at Mandasor.[1] The record opens with an invocation to the "*Purusha* with thousand heads (*sahasraśiras*) and immeasurable

[1] *Indian Antiquary*, 1913, '*Epigraphic notes and Questions*' by Dr. D. R. Bhandarkar; H. P. Śāstrī, Ep. Ind., XII, pp. 315 ff.

soul (*amitātman*) who sleeps on the waters of the four oceans as on a couch (*chatussamudra-paryaṅka-toya-nidrālu*).'' It is dated in the (Mālava) year 461 (404 A.D.), ''the festival of Śakra (Indra) having commenced, then allowed by Krishṇa (*Krishṇasyā-numata*),'' and extols a person named Satya ''whose wealth and life were dedicated to gods and Brāhmaṇas'' and who finding this world (*Jīvaloka*) to be transitory like the water of the mirage (*mṛigatṛishṇā*), like a dream, like the lightning and the flame of a lamp, took refuge (*śaraṅam gataḥ*) in Vāsudeva, the grantor of protection (*śaraṅya*), the abode of the world (*jagad vāsa*), the immeasurable (*aprameya*), the unborn (*aja*) and all-pervading (*vibhu*) ; who is further compared to a tree that gives heaven (*tridaśa*) as its noble fruit, whose charming young shoots are the celestial damsels, whose many branches are the heavenly cars (*vimāna*), and which drops honey in the shape of rains from the clouds. The Gaṅg-dhāra Inscription of the time of Viśvavarman, the son of Naravarman, records the erection, ''when there is the time of the awakening from sleep of Madhusūdana,'' of a temple of Vishṇu by Mayūrā-kshaka, one of the king's ministers, who displayed the most extreme devotion (*Parā bhakti*) to *Chakra-gadādhara*, wielder of the discus and club, *i.e.*, Vishṇu. The coins of the *Traikūṭaka* King Dahra-sena, the son of Indradatta, describe him as *Paramavaishṇava*. From a copper-plate found at

Pardi, south of Surat, we learn that Dabrasena flourished about A.D. 456.[1]

Some of the great Gupta sovereigns of Magadha describe themselves as "*paramabhāgavata*," and were unquestionably great champions of the religion of Vāsudeva. With the rise of their power Bhāgavatism, which was now synonymous with Vaishṇavism, naturally came to the forefront and spread to the remotest corners of India. The general prevalence of the religion throughout the Gupta Empire is attested by numerous inscriptions and sculptures. The Udayagiri Cave Inscription of the year 82 of the Gupta Era records the dedication of two images, one of Vishṇu, the other of a twelve-armed goddess who must be some form of Lakshmī, by a *mahārāja* of the *Sanakānika* family; the last component—'*ḍhala*' of his name alone is legible, but he is described as the son of *Mahārāja* Vishṇudāsa, and the grandson of the Mahārāja Chhagalaga; he refers to himself as *Śrī Chandraguptapādānudhyāta*, so that he must have been a feudatory of Chandra Gupta II Vikramāditya. The name of the father of—'*ḍhala*,' Vishṇudāsa, "Slave of Vishṇu," possibly indicates that he, too, was a *Bhāgavata* or *Vaishṇava*. The Bhitarī Pillar Inscription of Skanda Gupta records the installation of an image of *Śārṅgin*, the wielder of

[1] J.R.A.S., 1905, pp. 801-804.

the bow called Śārṅga, *i.e.*, Vishṇu, and the allotment to it of a village by the emperor in memory of his father Kumāra Gupta I, and to increase his merit. The inscription mentions Skanda Gupta's struggles with the Pushyamitras. Kumāra Gupta seems to have died before the success of his son's arms had been assured and the ruined fortunes of the family re-established ; it was therefore to his mother that the victorious prince returned to announce his victory, "just as Kṛishṇa, when he had slain his enemies, betook himself to (his mother) Devakī." The Junāgaḍh Inscription of the same reign contains an adoration of Vishṇu "the perpetual abode of Lakshmī, whose dwelling is the water-lily ; the conqueror of distress ; the completely victorious one, who, for the sake of the happiness of the lord of gods, seized back from Bali the goddess of wealth and splendour, who is admitted to be worthy of enjoyment and who had been kept away from him for a long time." The inscription records the erection of a temple of *Chakrabhṛit* (the wielder of the discus, *i.e.*, Kṛishṇa), by Chakrapālita who was the son of a governor of Skanda Gupta, and was a devoted worshipper of Govinda. Another inscription of the time of Skanda Gupta, *viz.*, the Gadhwā Inscription of 467-68 A.D., records the installation of an image of *Anantasvāmin* (Vishṇu) and a grant of some land at a village belonging to the same god under the name of *Chitrakūṭasvāmin*. The Eraṇ Stone

Pillar Inscription of the time of Budha Gupta contains an invocation of the all-pervading (*vibhu*), four-armed (deity) Janārdana, *i.e.*, Vishṇu, whose couch is the broad waters of the four oceans; who is the cause of the continuance, the production, and the destruction, etc., of the universe; (and) whose ensign (*ketu*) is Garuḍa. The epigraph records the erection of a *dhvajastambha* or flagstaff of the deity by the Mahārāja Mātṛivishṇu who is described as *atyanta-bhagavad-bhakta* "excessively devoted to the Blessed One." Another Eraṇ inscription executed in the reign of the Hun King Toramāṇa contains an adoration of the Boar Incarnation and records the erection of a stone temple of "Nārāyaṇa who has the form of a boar," by Dhanya-vishṇu, the younger brother of Mātṛivishṇu. A Dāmodarpur Copper-plate Inscription of the time of Budha Gupta is concerned with the construction of a temple for the god Śvetavarāhasvāmin and another Gupta epigraph of A D. 543-44 refers to provision for its repair.

After the disintegration of the empire of the Guptas the *Bhāgavata* or *Vaishṇava* religion flourished in the dominions of many of their former feudatories, especially in Central India. The Barabar Hill Cave Inscription of Anantavarman records the installation in the cave of an image of Kṛishṇa. The Khoh Copper-plate Inscription of the Parivrājaka Mahārāja Saṁkshoba (209 G. S. = 529 A.D.) contains an invocation of Vāsudeva, and records the gift of a village for the purpose of observing the *bali*, *charu* and *sattra* at the temple which the king had caused to be built for the goddess Pishṭapurī, probably a form of Lakshmī. The Khoh Copper-plate Inscription of Jayanātha records the gift of a village for the purpose of a temple of Vishṇu. Two inscriptions of the same place but executed in the reign of Śarvanātha record the gift of several villages for the purpose of the worship of the goddess Pishṭapurikā.

We learn from the Māliyā Copper-plate Inscription of Dharasena II that Dhruvasena I, King of Valabhī, was a *Bhāgavata* or *Vaishṇava*. The Alînā Copper-plate Inscription of Śîlâditya VII of the same dynasty refers to the man-lion (*Narasiṁha*) Incarnation. The Sārnāth Stone Inscription of Prakaṭāditya records the building of a temple to *Muradvish* (Vishṇu-Krishṇa). A temple of Deogarh, in the Lalitpur Subdivision of the Jhānsi district in the United Provinces, is adorned with sculptures which, according to V. Smith, may date from the first half of the sixth century A.D. The subject of one of these is Vishṇu as the Eternal, reclining on the serpent Ananta with the other gods watching from above. A composition nearly life-size, at Pathārî in the Bhopāl Agency, believed to represent the new-born Kṛishṇa lying by the side of his mother, who is watched by five attendants, is considered by some to be the finest and largest piece of Indian sculpture.[1] The style, says Smith, is much the same as that of the Deogarh panels, and the group must be of nearly the same age.

We shall now try to find out the most salient features of "Guptan Vaishṇavism." The records of the Gupta Age refer to the close association of Bhāgavatism with *Yoga* philosophy and solar worship, which is also noticed in the *Gītā* and the *Nārāyaṇīya*.[2] It is clear from the Tuśām Inscription that the *Sātvatas* or the *Bhāgavatas* had now definitely accepted the identification of their Kṛishṇa with Vishṇu. Vishṇu's epithet "The mighty bee on the water-lily which is the face of Jāmbavatī" certainly refers to Kṛishṇa who is, in the *Purāṇas* and the *Mahā-Ummagga Jātaka*,[3] the husband of Jāmbavatī or Jambāvatī.[4] But though Kṛishṇa and Vishṇu were regarded as identical, the latter name was now the more usual designation of the Supreme God of the *Sātvatas* or the *Bhāgavatas*. Vishṇu, Purusha, Nārāyaṇa, Janārdana, was now the Supreme Deity. Kṛishṇa was merely his most perfect Incarnation. In other words, Bhāgavatism

1 See V. Smith's *History of Fine Art in India and Ceylon*, p. 164.

2 Fleet, Corpus Inscriptionum Indicarum, Vol. III, pp. 127, 270 (*Bhagavat-pādānām Āditya-bhaṭṭāraka-pādānām cha*; *Sātvata-yogāchāryya-bhagavadbhakta*).

3 No. 546. The *Jātaka*, edited by Cowell, Vol. VI, pp. 216-17.

4 In the *Jātaka* Jāmbavatī is represented as a Chaṇḍāla maiden. The Gupta epigraphs make no mention of Rādhā who is referred to in Hāla's *Sapta-Śatakam* (Ind. Ant., 1874., 25 n.) and later works. For references to Kṛishṇa as *Rādhāvirahātura* and *Rādhādhava* see *op. cit.*, 1877, p. 51; 1893, p. 82.

had now lost itself in Vishṇuism. The earth is *Vaishṇavī*, belonging to Vishṇu. It is Vishṇu who, for the sake of Indra, seized back from Bali the goddess Śrī. It is Purusha who, according to the Allahabad *Praśasti* of Samudra Gupta, caused *Udaya* (creation) and *Pralaya* (destruction) and, according to a Mandasor inscription, slept on the waters of the four oceans as on a couch. It is the *Bhagavat* Nārāyaṇa who, according to an Eraṇ Inscription, became incarnate as a Boar "to lift up the earth and to serve as the pillar for the support of the great house which is the three worlds." It is Janārdana who, according to another Eraṇ epigraph, lay on the broad waters of the four oceans and is the cause of the continuance, the production and the destruction of the universe. In the concluding portion of the Mandasor record of Naravarman, however, the Supreme deity receives the name Vāsudeva and is described in terms which remind us of the *Bhagavad Gītā*. He is *Śaraṇya* (refuge of beings), *Jagadvāsa* (home of the universe), *Aprameya* (the immeasurable), *Aja* (unborn), and *Vibhu* (all-pervading). People leaving the world and its fleeting joys take shelter in him (*Śaraṇāgata*). But the heaven (*tridaśa*) of the Mandasor record is too earthly to bear comparison with the *param sthānam* of the Lord's Song.

Along with Kṛishṇa there appear other beings who are also regarded as incarnations of Vishṇu-

Nārāyaṇa. The worship of the incarnations is a notable feature of the Vaishṇavism of the Gupta period. The Boar Incarnation is expressly referred to in the Eraṇ Inscription of the time of Toramāṇa and some of the Dāmodarpur plates. The Dwarf Incarnation is clearly implied in the statement of the Junāgaḍh Inscription :—"who, for the sake of the happiness of the lord of the gods, seized back from Bali the goddess of wealth and splendour." The man-lion incarnation is mentioned in the Alînā plate. The Rāma *Avatāra* is not referred to in any of the Gupta inscriptions, but is mentioned by Kālidāsa[1] (*Rāmābhidhāno Hari*) who probably belonged to the Gupta age. The Rāma cult however was still in its infancy. A *Rāmatîrtha* (place of pilgrimage) is mentioned in a Nasik cave inscription of the second century A.D. But it is difficult to say whether it was named after the Rāghava prince, as the son of Jamadagni and the elder brother of Vāsudeva bore the same name. Rāma worship was certainly favoured by some of the early Tamil saints, notably Kulaśekhara, and Varāhamihira in his *Bṛihat-Saṁhitā*[2] refers to images of Rāma, son of Daśaratha. But there is no clear evidence of the existence of a Ramaite sect before the age of Rāmānanda. The germs of the Dwarf, the Boar, the Fish and the Tortoise *Avatāras* are to

1 *Raghuvaṁśa*, xiii, 1.
2 LVIII, 29-30.

be found in the *Śatapatha* and a few other *Brāhmaṇas* but not as yet connected with Vishṇu (the Dwarf alone excepted). Nṛisiṁha appears in the *Taittirīya Āraṇyaka*. In a notable passage of the *Nārāyaṇīya*,[1] only the Boar, the Dwarf, the Man-Lion and Man (Vāsudeva?) appear as *avatāras*. In a second list[2] two more, Rāma Bhārgava and Rāma Dāśarathi, are added. In a third list[3] Haṁsa, Kūrma, Matsya, and Kalkī are added, while in the Matsya Purāṇa[4] and the Bhāgavata Purāṇa[5] Buddha appears in the list of the *Avatāras*. The last mentioned work raises the number of Avatāras to twenty-three and includes even Ṛishabha, probably the first Tīrthaṅkara of the Jainas. The *Ahirbudhnya Saṁhitā* speaks of thirty-nine *Vibhavas* or manifestations of the Supreme Being and includes in the list not only some of the well-known *Avatāras* but also Kapila and Nara. The *Vishvaksena Saṁhitā* refers to secondary *Avatāras* and cites as instances Buddha, Arjuna and others. The doctrine of the Avatāras thus underwent several stages of development.

With the worship of the *Avatāras* may be contrasted the almost total absence of any reference to the *Vyūhas* Saṅkarshaṇa, Pradyumna and Aniruddha

1 Mbh., xii, 349, 37.
2 *Op. cit.*, 339, 77-90.
3 *Op. cit.*, 339, 104.
4 47, 247.
5 1, 3, 24.

in the inscriptions of the Gupta Age. The *Vyūhas* as well as the ten Avatāras are met with in the *Nārāyaṇīya.* The *Mahābhāshya* of Patañjali and the Ghosuṇḍī and Nānāghāt Inscriptions show that the cult of the Vyūhas in some shape must have prevailed in the second and first centuries B.C. The disappearance of the independent worship of the *Vyūhas* excepting Vāsudeva was perhaps one of the first fruits of the growing popularity of the *Avatāras.* The ousting of the *Vyūhas* by the *Avatāras* was one of the characteristic signs of the transformation of Bhāgavatism into Vishṇuism.[1]

Another important feature of the Vaishṇavism of the Gupta period was the worship of Lakshmī. Under the name of Sirimā Devatā Lakshmī appears to have been worshipped by the Brāhmaṇical Hindus and Buddhists alike before the Christian era. We have representations, of a very early date, of this goddess on the Bhārhut Tope, and on certain silver coins of the Mahākshatrapa Rājuvula of Mathurā.[2] She had only a minor place in the early Vishṇuite pantheon.[3] But, as Sister

[1] The adoration of Saṅkarshaṇa and Vāsudeva seems to survive in a modified form in the worship of "Bala, Kṛishṇa and Subhadrā" mentioned in a Bhubaneśwara inscription (Ep. Ind., XIII, 153). Varāhamihira (LVIII, 36 37) refers to images of Baladeva and Kṛishṇa standing on either side of *Ekānaṁsā* (Subhadrā ?) who is identified with Pārvatī by the *Trikāṇḍaśesha* and the *Śabda Kalpadruma.*

[2] Rhys Davids, *Buddhist India,* pp. 216-219, and Cunningham, *Coins of Ancient India,* p. 86.

[3] *Cf. Bodhāyana Dharmasūtra,* ii, 5, 24.

Niveditā has pointed out,[1] "a great formative movement took place in the history of Vaishṇavism when India was united under the Guptas." The "enthronement of Lakshmī beside Nārāyaṇa as the centre of Vaishṇava worship" [2] is not an isolated fact. It is paralleled by the prominent position held by the *Devīs* or royal consorts in the inscriptions and on the coins of the Gupta Emperors. There is reason to believe that there was "a strong movement for the assertion of the rights of woman" [3] in the Gupta period. The influence of the *Sāṅkhya* doctrine of *Purusha* and *Prakṛiti* on the neo-Vaishṇavism may also be detected in the Lakshmī-Nārāyaṇa cult. The numismatic evidence seems to point to the fact that the worship of Pallas and other Greek goddesses had something to do with the wide diffusion of the cult of Śrī. On Rājuvula's coin mentioned above Lakshmī sometimes takes the place of Pallas on the reverse.

Side by side with Lakshmī appears another goddess, Bhūdevī, or the Earth, who is called *Vaishṇavī*, consort of Vishṇu, in several records of east central India.[4]

In a previous lecture I have adduced grounds for believing that the principal *Purāṇas* were

[1] *Footfalls of Indian History*, p. 213.

[2] *Op. cit.*, p. 206.

[3] *Op. cit.*, p. 206.

[4] Fleet, Corpus Inscriptionum Indicarum, Vol. III, pp. 194, 198, 296.

composed or compiled during the Gupta Age. But it is not safe to depend on them in writing the history of ancient Vaishṇavism. The *Purāṇas* have been added to from time to time and the texts have undergone such corruption that no one can be positively certain that a particular chapter was not interpolated in comparatively recent times. *E.g.*, the *Vāyu Purāṇa* known to the *Mahābhārata* [1] was different from our present text. The passages from the *Purāṇa* quoted in the epic do not agree with the corresponding passages of the extant work. What is true of the *Vāyu* is also true of the *Matsya*, *Vishṇu*, *Bhāgavata* and *Brahma-Vaivartta* Purāṇas. The great Bengali writer, Bankimchandra, shows in his *Kṛishṇa-Charitra* that the contents of the extant *Brahma-Vaivartta Purāṇa* do not agree with the contents of the work given in the *Matsya*. As the extant *Purāṇa* texts are unreliable I have generally abstained from using them in the present historic sketch and have depended mainly on the sure guidance of epigraphy.

With the fall of the Guptas Bhāgavatism lost its pre-eminence in Northern India. The most powerful sovereigns of the next period, *e.g.*, Mihiragula, Yaśodharman and Harsha, were adherents of non-*Bhāgavata* creeds. But there is reason to believe that though hurled from its eminent

1 iii, 191, 16, *Vāyuproktamanusmṛitya Purāṇam Ṛishi-saṁstutam.*

position, it was far from being extinct in Northern India. The *Bṛihat Saṁhitā* of Varāhamihira refers to *Bhaktas* of Vāsudeva [1] and defines *Bhāgavata* as one devoted to the worship of Vishṇu.[2] In the *Harsha-charita* of Bāṇabhaṭṭa (seventh century A.D.) King Harsha is represented as meeting not only Buddhists and Jainas but also *Bhāgavatas*. Bāṇa mentions not only the *Bhāgavatas* but also the *Pañcharātras*. The word *Pañcharātra* was sometimes used as a synonym of *Bhāgavata* ; more often it designated an important branch of the *Bhāgavata* sect.[3] Schrader believes that some of the *Pañcharātra Saṁhitās* were composed in Kaśmîra between the fourth and eighth centuries A.D. Magnificent temples in honour of Vaishṇava deities were constructed in Kaśmîra in the reign of Avantivarman.[4]

The *Bhāgavatas* were an influential sect in the early part of the ninth century A.D. Śaṅkarāchārya in a well-known passage of his commentary on the *Brahmasūtras* [5] combats the *Bhāgavata* doctrine (which he calls *Pañcharātra*) and asserts its incompleteness and unorthodoxy. The passage seems to intimate that the promulgator of the *Pañcharātra* system was Śāṇḍilya, who was

[1] LXIX, 32.
[2] LX, 19.
[3] Ind. Ant., 1908, p. 258.
[4] Rājataraṅgiṇī, V, 23-30.
[5] II, ii, 42-45.

dissatisfied with the Vedas, not finding in them prompt and sufficient way of supreme excellence (*Para-śreyas*) and final beatitude; and therefore he had recourse to this *Śāstra*. Śāṇḍilya was probably one of the first among those who systematised the doctrines of the *Vāsudevakas*. If we regard him as identical with Udara Śāṇḍilya of the Vedic texts, he is tenth in the apostolic succession from Indrota,[1] the priest of Janamejaya, the great-grandson of Kṛishṇa's sister Subhadrā.

Though the *Bhāgavata* religion still flourished in the north, its stronghold was now not the valley of the Ganges or Central India, but the Tamil country. There the faith flourished under the strong impetus given by the Āḷvārs "who by their Tamil songs inculcated *Bhakti* and Kṛishṇa-worship mainly." Bhāgavatism had penetrated into the Deccan at least as early as the first century B.C.[2] The China inscription of the time of Yajña Sātakarṇi shows that the faith flourished in the Kṛishṇā District in the second century A.D. In the sixth century A.D. the Chalukya king Maṅgaleśa is described as a *parama bhāgavata* or most devout worshipper of the Blessed One and bas reliefs at Badami belonging to this period depict many scenes connected with Kṛishṇa and other deities of the Vishṇuite pantheon. The

1 *Vaṁśa Brāhmaṇa*, 2.

2 *Cf.* the Nānāghāṭ Inscription.

significant name "Vishṇu gopa" of Kāñchī found in the Allahabad *Praśasti* of Samudra Gupta probably indicates that the Kṛishṇa cult had found its way to the extreme south before the middle of the fourth century A.D. Nay, we have a more direct evidence of the existence of Kṛishṇa-Baladeva worship in the Tamil country in the early centuries of the Christian era. The *Chilappathikaram* (*Śilappadikāram*) and the other ancient Tamil poems refer to temples dedicated to Kṛishṇa and his brother at Madurā, Kāviripaddinam and other cities.[1] The poet Kari-kannam of Kāviripaddinam described the two kings Karikal and Velli-ampala-thu-Thunjia-Peru-Valuthi as "majestic like the two gods one of whom fair in complexion, bears the flag of the palmyra (Baladeva) and the other of dark hue, whose weapon is a wheel.[2] The wide prevalence of Bhāgavatism in the Far South is also testified to by the *Bhāgavata Purāṇa* which says[3] that in the Kali Age devoted worshippers of Nārāyaṇa, though rare in some places, are to be found in large numbers in the Draviḍa country watered by the rivers Tāmraparṇī, Kṛitamālā, the sacred Kāverī and the great stream (Periyār ?) flowing to the west. Pure souls who

[1] Kanakasabhai's "*The Tamils Eighteen Hundred Years Ago*," pp. 13, 26.

[2] Kanakasabhai's "*The Tamils Eighteen Hundred Years Ago*," pp. 68-69.

[3] xi, 5, 38 ff.

drink the water of these streams are usually devoted to the Blessed Vāsudeva (*Prāyo bhaktā Bhagavati Vāsudeve 'malâśayāḥ*).

The Vaishṇava tradition of Southern India mentions twelve Āḷvārs,[1] namely :—

1. Poygai or Poykai Āḷvār.
2. Bhūtattār (Āḷvār).
3. Pey Āḷvār.
4. Tirumaḷiśai Āḷvār.
5. Namm-Āḷvār or saint Śaṭakopa.
6. Mathura Kavi or Madhurakavi Āḷvār.
7. Kulaśekhara Āḷvār.
8. Periy-Āḷvār or Vishṇuchitta.
9. Āṇḍāl.
10. Toṇḍaraḍippoḍi Āḷvār.
11. Tiruppāṇ Āḷvār.
12. Tirumaṅgai Āḷvār.

The word Āḷvār literally means "those who are immersed (in devotion to or love of god)." These saints came from both sexes and from many castes including the lowest. They composed the *Divya Prabandham* or *Nālāyira Prabandham, i.e.*,

[1] For the Āḷvārs see S. Krishnaswami Aiyangar, *Sri Rāmānujāchārya*, pp. 4 ff. ; T. Rājagopālāchāriar, *The Vaishṇavite Reformers of India*, pp. 2, 138 ff. ; Sir R. G. Bhandarkar, *Vaiṣṇavism, etc.*, pp. 48 ff. ; Dikshitar, *Studies in Tamil Literature and History*, pp. 103 ff. ; J. S. M. Hooper, *Hymns of the Āḷvārs*; Farquhar, *An Outline of the Religious Literature of India*, pp. 187 f. ; K. G. Sesha Aiyar, I.H.Q. 1931, pp. 724 ff. Pandit M. Raghava Aiyangar, *The Contemporaneity of Saints Tirumangaiyar and Gnanasambandha* (Dr. S. K. Aiyangar Commemoration Volume, 201 ff.), etc.

the collection of four thousand lyrics of divine praise. The songs were gathered together by Nāthamuni, the famous Āchārya, who probably lived in the eleventh century A.D. The three earliest Āḷvārs were mythical in their origin and are said to have been born at Kāñchī, Mahābalipuram and Mylapore respectively. They are represented as having met at the modern Tirukkoilur, where they had a vision of God and poured forth their joy at the sight in Tamil verses of a hundred each. These saints speak of Nārāyaṇa as the Supreme Divinity, refer frequently to the early *Avatāras* or descents of Vishṇu, especially the *Trivikrama*, and are eloquent in their praise of the Kṛishṇa *Avatāra*. They show acquaintance with the principal *Purāṇas* and worship images of the more ancient temples of the Tamil country, like those at Śrîraṅgam, Tirupati, and Alagarkoil. They speak with reverence of the Vedic canon but teach the adoration of the Deity by recitation of His names, services at the shrines and meditation on His personal forms. Tirumaḷiśai Āḷvār was the next in the traditional list. He was born in the hamlet of Tirumaḷiśai, near Poonamallee and lived for some time at Kāñchī. "Those who will not worship Vishṇu," says he in his hymns, "are low indeed." The fifth Āḷvār Saint Śaṭagopa, Śaṭakopa or Namm-Āḷvār stands first among the Āḷvārs in order of importance. He wrote the *Tiruviruttam*, the *Tiruvāśiriam*, the *Periya Tiru vandādi* and another work that has the distinctive appellation *Tiruvāymoḻi*, "the word of the mouth." He was the son of a Pāṇḍya chieftain and his native city was Kurukai or Kurukūr near modern Tinnevelly on the Tāmraparṇī. He composed over a thousand stanzas in classical Tamil. He preached ecstatic love to the Lord conceived of as *Nāyaka* or lover with the devotee as his beloved. Mathurakavi or Madhurakavi was a Brāhmaṇa of Tirukkovilūr. He was a worshipper of his *Guru* exclusively. Kulaśekhar Āḷvār was a ruler of ancient Kerala on the Malabar coast. He composed songs in praise of Mahāvishṇu and his favourite *avatāra* was Śrī Rāmachandra. The section of the *Prabandham* consisting of his songs is called *Perumāḻ-Tirumoḻi*. Periy-Āḷvār or Vishṇuchitta, was born at Śrī Villiputtūr. He was a composer of extensive songs. Among these the most famous is the *Tiruppallāṇḍu*. The Āḷvār also wrote the *Tirumoḻi* which is concerned with the exploits of Kṛishṇa. Āṇḍāl Kodāi or Nāchchiyār was a lady, the reputed daughter of Vishṇuchitta, who may rightly be called the "Mīrā Bāi" of the South. She was probably born about A.D. 716. She expresses passionate longing for Kṛishṇa whom she regards as her lover. The chief works attributed to her are the *Tiruppāvai muppatu* and the *Nāchchiyār Tirumoḻi* (The sacred speech of the queen). Toṇḍaraḍippoḍi ("the Dust of the Feet of the Slaves of God"), the next Āḷvār, known originally as Vipra Nārāyaṇa, was a native of Maṇḍaṅguḍi. His favourite deity was Raṅganātha at Śrīraṅgam. He wrote the sacred poems known as the *Tirumālai* (the sacred garland) and the *Tiruppai Yeuchiḷḷ* (the Rousing of the Lord).

Tiruppāṇ, the eleventh Āḷvār, was the adopted child of a lute-player at Uraiyur near Trichinopoly. He composed the *Amalan-ādipirān* in ten stanzas.

The last of the Āḷvārs is Tirumaṅgai who is the author of the largest number (1,361) of the four thousand verses of the Tamil Vaishṇava *Prabandham*. Tirumaṇgai belonged to the Kallar caste and was born at Tiruvāli Tirunagari or Kurugur in the Tanjore district. He served under the Chola kiṇg and afterwards lived in Śrīraṅgam and rebuilt some parts of the great shrine, the funds for which he had to find by robbing the great Buddhist establishment at Negapataṃ of its golden image of the Śākya sage. He provided for the recital of Namm-Āḷvār's *Tiruvāymoli* annually at Śrīraṅgam. The date of this Āḷvār is a subject on which opinion is divided. Bishop Caldwell held that he was a disciple of Rāmānuja, while Gopīnāth Rāo is willing to believe that he was a contemporary, if not actually a disciple, of Yāmunāchārya Ālavandār, Rāmānuja's great-grandfaṭher and predecessor in the apostolic succession of Vaishṇavism, who lived in the eleventh century A.D.[1]

[1] Farquhar, *Rel. Lit.*, 379; Ind. Ant., 1906, p. 230.

It is however clear from the centum known as the *Rāmānujanūrrandhādhi*, a work composed during the lifetime of Rāmānujāchārya by Amudan, a convert and pupil of one of the great Āchārya's own disciples, that Rāmānuja lived long after Tirumaṅgai, and had read and derived much wisdom from the works of that Āḻvār.[1] That the last Āḻvār was not a disciple, or contemporary, of Yāmunāchārya is proved by a stanza in praise of his work by Tirukkoṭṭiyūr Nambi, a teacher of Rāmānuja and, therefore, a contemporary of Yāmuna. The eulogium goes to show that Tirumaṅgai's works had been regularly studied and handed down from preceptor to disciple for some time at least. A decad of Tirumaṅgai in praise of the Paramesvara Vinnagara at Kāñchī gives in great detail the achievements of a Pallava ruler whom Dr. Hultzsch considers to be identical with Paramesvara Varman II, from the name of the shrine. This, says Krishṇaswāmī Aiyaṅgar[2] is not a necessary inference, as any other Pallava paramount sovereign might have had the title Pallava Paramesvara. The details given in the decad do not find support from what is known of Paramesvara Varman II. There is a story that Tirumaṅgai held a successful disputation with the Saiva saint Tiruñāna Sambandar, supposed to

[1] S. Krishṇaswāmi Aiyangar, *Ancient India*, p. 407.

[2] Ind. Ant., 1906, p. 231.

be a contemporary of the celebrated Pallava ruler Narasiṁha Varman I of Kāñchī who reigned about A.D. 642. The date of the Śaiva saint has then to be allotted to the middle of the seventh century A.D. The date of his Vaishṇava contemporary must in that case fall either in the middle of the seventh century, or, if he was a younger contemporary, in the latter part of the same century and the beginning of the eighth. Mr. V. R. Ramchandra Dikshitar, following the late Gopīnātha Rao, however, points out that Tirumangai refers to Pallavamalla and Vayiramega who are identified with Nandi Varman Pallavamalla and his Rāshṭrakūṭa contemporary Dantidurga who flourished about the middle of the eighth century A.D. The Āḷvār, according to this view, could not have flourished before *c.* 750 A.D.

The dates (4203-2706 B.C.) assigned by the "hagiologists" to the earlier Āḷvārs do not bear scrutiny. Since the Āḷvār mentioned last in the traditional list lived in or about the eighth century A.D., it is surmised that the earliest saints must have lived long before this period, possibly in the opening years of the Christian era. But the matter is not free from doubt. In the opinion of the late Gopīnātha Rao, Bhūtattāḷvār, the second saint, who makes reference to Māmallai or Mahābalipuram, a city named after Narasimha-Varman I, surnamed Mahāmalla, could not have lived earlier than the seventh century A.D. The same remark applies to his traditional contemporaries, the first, third and fourth Āḷvārs. Mr. V. R. Ramchandra Dikshitar suggests [1] that Nammāḷvār, too, may be placed in the seventh century, though many other scholars including Gopīnātha Rao are inclined to assign to him a much later date. Kulaśekhara is placed by Sir Ramkrishna Bhandarkar in the twelfth century A.D., while Mr. K. G. Sesha Aiyar assigns to him a date in the sixth century on reasons that are not very convincing.[2] Epigraphic evidence suggests that the Āḷvār flourished some time before Rājendra Chola I.[3] The commentatory verses in regard to some of his lyrics are written by Maṇakkāl Nambi who is said to have been born in the ninth century A.D.[4]

The Āḷvārs were followed by another group of teachers called Āchāryas [5] who represented the intellectual side of Tamilian Vaishṇavism as the Āḷvārs did the emotional side. The first of the Āchāryas was Nāthamuni or Raṅganāthāchārya. He was a native of Vîranārāyaṇapura, the modern Mannargudi, and was probably a descendant of

1 *Studies in Tamil Literature and History*, pp. 105-106.

2 *The Indian Historical Quarterly*, 1931, p. 734.

3 *Op. cit.*, p. 728.

4 *Op. cit.*, pp. 732-33.

5 For the *Āchāryas* see T. Rājagopālāchāriar, *The Vaishṇavite Reformers of India*, pp. 1 ff., 140 ff., *Srībhāshya* of Rāmānujāchārya. trans. by M. Raṅgāchārya and M. B. Varadarāja Aiyangar, Vol. I, pp. 89 ff., 158.

the early Vaishṇava immigrants from the North who carried the *Bhāgavata* cult to the Tamil country. He lived in the town of Śrīraṅgam near Trichinopoly probably during the eleventh century A.D. The traditional date of his death is 920 A.D. But if the story regarding his synchronism with a Chola king whose capital was Gangaikonda Cholapuram be correct [1] he could not have died earlier than the reign of Rājendra Chola I Gangaikonda (eleventh century A.D.).

Nāthamuni was a passionate lover of the songs of the Āḷvārs, especially of Śaṭakopa. He is said to have recovered the whole of Śaṭakopa's works and to have arranged them and the extant works of the other Āḷvārs into four collections of almost a thousand stanzas each. He also composed a Sanskrit work, the *Nyāyatattva*, extracts from which are given in the *Nyāyasiddhāñjana* of Śrī Vedānta Deśika, a famous Vaishṇava writer of the fourteenth century A.D. The *Nyāyatattva*, in the opinion of T. Rājagopālāchāriar, was an elaborate treatise covering the whole field of philosophy from the point of view of the *Viśishṭādvaita* school. The doctrine peculiar to the school of which Nāthamuni was the founder, and Rāmānuja the great exponent, is that of *Prapatti* or surrender to God in absolute renunciation and faith. The doctrine is founded on the *Bhagavad Gītā*

1 T. Rājagopālāchāriar, *The Vaishṇavite Reformers of India*, p. 7.

and the older *Pañcharātra Tantras*, and is a cardinal doctrine of the Vaishṇava. In the *Gītā* [1] we are told that it is only those who surrender themselves to (*Prapadyante*) the Blessed Vāsudeva that receive divine grace and pass beyond the bounds of *māyā*. Such persons are called *Prapanna*.[2] *Prapatti* is also dealt with in the *Bhāradvāja Saṁhitā*.[3] It is said to have been accepted and brought into practice by Nammāḷvār, and by Nāthamuni after him. It was elaborated by Rāmānuja's successors. In his later days Nāthamuni made a pilgrimage to the most sacred spots in the Vaishṇava Holy Land, including Mathurā, the Bethlehem of Bhāgavatism. It was in commemoration of this visit, with his son and daughter-in-law, to the banks of the Yamunā, that his grandson is said to have been named Yāmuna.

Nāthamuni infused fresh energy into the heart of Vaishṇavism, and the sect of Śrîvaishṇavas established by him was destined to have a chequered career in the annals of India.

The second *Āchārya* was Puṇḍarîkāksha who is said to have been born at Tiruvallari, north of Śrîraṅgam. He received from his guru Nāthamuni, the name of *Uyyakkondar* or Saviour of the New Dispensation.

1 IV, 11; VII, 14.

2 *Op. cit.*, II, 7.

3 Schrader, *Introduction to the Pañcharātra*, p. 23.

Rāmamiśra was the next in the apostolic succession after Puṇḍarîkāksha. He does not appear to have been a man of strong personality like Nāthamuni, but he had the enthusiasm of his predecessors and holds an honourable place among the Vaishṇava apostles as the spiritual instructor of the great Yāmunāchārya Āḷavandār.

"Yāmunāchārya," says T. Rājagopālāchāriar, "really laid the foundation for all the doctrines that go under Rāmānuja's name." Yāmuna was born in the city of Vîranārāyaṇapura(the modern Mannargudi in the South Arcot District) in the palmy days of Chola imperialism. He was the son of Īśvara Bhaṭṭa, and the grandson of Nāthamuni.

Yāmuna first distinguished himself by vanquishing one Akki Alwan, the Court Pundit of the reigning Chola king, in a *Śāstric* disputation, and was hailed by the Chola queen as Ālavandār or the Victor. He was granted some lands by the king and lived a life of pleasure and luxury. The story goes that one day Rāmamiśra managed to gain an interview with him and persuaded him to visit the shrine of Śrîraṅgam to receive a valuable treasure which Nāthamuni had left for his grandson. When he reached the temple Yāmuna was told that the treasure was the Deity Himself. His eyes were now opened. He took up his residence at Śrîraṅgam and devoted himself to the task of expounding the doctrines of the Viśishṭādvaita school which is "a somewhat modified and more methodical form of the ancient *Bhāgavata, Pañcharātra*, or *Sātvata* religion."

The most important work of Yāmunāchārya is the *Siddhitraya*. It contains three sections called the *Ātma-Siddhi*, the *Īśvara Siddhi* and the *Saṁvit Siddhi*, and is said to have for its object the demonstration of the real existence of the individual and Supreme souls, and the refutation of the doctrine of *Avidyā*. The *Siddhitraya* is quoted frequently by Rāmānuja.

Another important work of Yāmunāchārya is the *Āgamaprāmāṇya* which maintains the orthodoxy of the *Bhāgavata* or *Pañcharātra* school against the attack of Śaṅkarāchārya.

Yāmunāchārya is also the author of the *Gītārthasaṁgraha* which contains a summary of the teachings of the *Bhagavad gītā*. Following antecedent oral teaching he analysed the Divine Song as a consistent exposition of the doctrine of *Bhakti* supplemented by a description of the *Karma* and *Jñāna Yogas* as subordinate to the main theme.

Among other works of Yāmunācharya may be mentioned the *Mahāpurushanirṇaya* and the *Stotraratna*. The *Stotraratna* has been commented upon by the great *Vaishṇava* writer Śrî Vedānta Deśika. "Its spirit of earnest piety," says Dr. Macnicol, "may be taken as indicative of the real religious value of this Vaishṇavism of the South."

Yāmunāchārya's is thus one of the greatest names in the whole history of the Vaishṇavite development. It is said by some historians that, had there been no Philip, there would have been no Alexander ; it may perhaps be said with greater precision that had there been no Yāmunāchārya there would have been no Rāmānuja. The great prophet of mediæval Vaishṇavism has had to follow in the lines laid down by the great apostle who wrote the *Siddhitraya* and the *Āgamaprāmāṇya*.

Yāmunāchārya is said to have died in the eleventh century A.D., having expressed a wish to see Rāmānuja established at Śrîraṅgam as his spiritual successor. The wish was duly carried out, and the school founded by Nāthamuni and raised to eminence by Yāmunāchārya was strengthened by the advent of the man who may be looked upon as the second founder of Vaishṇavism, who "accomplished for Indian Theism, a work similar to that which the Greek Fathers did for Christianity in its Hellenic environment."

Having given a brief account of the lives of the Tamil *Āchāryas* to whom Rāmānuja owed so much, I proceed to note the special features of the religion which they professed and preached.

In the first place the new school, called the *Śrī Vaishṇava* or *Viśishṭādvaita* school, tacitly discarded the *Karma-mārga* of the *Mīmāṁsā* philosophers according to which salvation may be attained by the sole means of the faithful performance of *Karma* or the periodical ceremonial rites enjoined by the *Vedas* and the *Smṛitis*. *Śrī Vaishṇavism*, like the school of Śaṅkara, was in one respect the expression of a natural reaction from the sacrifice-ridden *Pūrva Mīmāṁsā* schools of Prabhākara, Kumārila Bhaṭṭa, Maṇḍana Miśra and others, which were in their turn the outcome of the disgust at the development of atheistic Buddhism.[1] The Vaishṇavas, while abstaining from an open denunciation of the *Karma Kāṇḍa*, disapproved of all *Karma* which is done for worldly or transient results and considered that the best antidote to its evil effects is the renunciation of all attachment to the fruits thereof.

Śrī Vaishṇavism was also a protest against the system of Śaṅkara. The great *Advaita* philosopher laid unusual stress on *Jñāna*. Even among the most learned in Śaṅkara's school a tendency was seen to make religion "more an affair of the head than of the heart." In a system of Absolute Monism there is hardly any room for *Bhakti*, in the popular sense, as a feeling of reverence for a Being conceived as higher than the soul of the devotee. The *Śrī Vaishṇavas* attacked this system and explained the ancient scriptures in a far more human spirit than Śaṅkara did. In refuting the absolute identity doctrine derived by Śaṅkara from

[1] T. Rājagopālāchāriar, *The Vaishṇavite Reformers of India*, pp. 18 ff.

the *Upanishad* text '*Ekamevādvitīyam*,' Yāmunāchārya says :—

Yathā Chola nṛipaḥ samrāḍadvitīyo'sti bhūtale
Iti tattulyanṛipati-nivāraṇaparaṁ vachaḥ
Na tu tatputra-tadbhṛitya-kalatrādinivāraṇam

"To say that the Chola king, now reigning in this country, is all supreme and without a second, can only exclude the existence of another monarch equal (in power) to him ; it cannot imply the denial of the existence of a wife, sons or servants of such a monarch." [1]

The protest against Śaṅkara's system was carried further by Madhva, a Vaishṇava apostle of the thirteenth century A.D.

Śrī Vaishṇavism loosened the hold of its followers on the various minor gods who were propitiated with a view to the attainment of various worldly objects. Devotion to one Deity was the teaching of this school. The ordinary Indian is eclectic. The Śrī Vaishṇavite alone had something of the Hebrew spirit of exclusiveness. To the follower of Śaṅkara one Personal God was as good as another and both were simply of 'phenomenal importance.' But the Śrī Vaishṇavite like the Hebrew refused to recognise as objects of worship deities other than their own favourite.

1 T. Rājagopālāchāriar, *The Vaishṇavite Reformers of India*, p. 36.

Another remarkable characteristic of Vaishṇavism was its solicitude for the lower classes. Unlike the more orthodox forms of Hinduism, it did not keep the Śūdras and the untouchables at a distance, but brought them into its fold and extended to them the privilege of knowing God and of attaining liberation. The agencies employed in effecting this were :—(1) the doctrine of *prapatti* or surrender to God, which was conceived as demanding no caste status or educational qualification, (2) the adoption for religious purposes of the works of the Āḷvārs and making them the common property of all classes, Brāhmaṇas and non-Brāhmaṇas alike.

But although liberal in this respect the *Śrī Vaishṇava Āchāryas* firmly supported caste, eschewed all heresy, and upheld the *Śāstras*. The conservatism of the southern *Vaishṇavas* in social matters was productive of important consequences in later times. Rāmānanda, one of the apostolic successors of Rāmānuja, insulted by his brethren for his social inferiority,[1] returned to the north, the land of his birth,[2] and established the famous sect which can boast of a Kavīra and a Tulasī Dās.

[1] T. Rājagopālāchāriar, *The Vaishṇavite Reformers of India*, p. 145.

[2] Sir George Grierson points out that he was born at Prayāga (Allahabad) and was educated at Benares. *J.R.A.S.*, Oct., 1920, pp. 591 ff.

BIBLIOGRAPHIC INDEX *

	PAGE
Acta Orientalia	151
Âgamapramāṇya—Yāmunāchārya ...	192 ff
Ahirbudhnya Saṁhitā	3, 97, 122, 175
A History of Fine Art in India and Ceylon, Smith, V. A.	99, 146, 172
Aiyangar Commemoration Volume ...	182 ff
Alphabetum Tibetanum, P. Georgi (*Ind. Ant.*)	128
Anantagītā	85
Ancient India, Megasthenes and Arrian, McCrindle	38, 72, 94, 102
Ancient India, Rapson	29
Ancient India, S. K. Aiyangar ...	186
An Outline of the Religious Literature of India	182 ff
Anugītā	60, 85, 155
Āraṇyaka—	
—Aitareya, Ed. R. L. Mitra ...	26, 36
—Taittirîya, Ed. R. L. Mitra ...	3, 16, 30, 32, 107, 111 ff, 131, 148, 159, 175
Archæological Survey of India (Report) ...	99, 151, 163 ff
Archæology and Vaishṇava Tradition, Chanda	22
Arthaśāstra, Kauṭilya, R. Shāmaśāstry ...	4, 33, 65, 78, 96
Ashṭādhyāyî, Pāṇini, Ed. S. C. Vasu ...	3 ff *passim*, 101
Asiatic Researches	129

* Not exhaustive. See also Pp. 3 ff *ante*.

PAGE

Aśokāvadāna 39, 55
Aupapātika Sūtra—Leumann, Dr. Ernst 121
Awakening of Faith—Aśvaghosha ... 124 ff, 161

Beginnings of Buddhist Art, Foucher ... 148
Bhagavadgîtā ... 2 ff *passim*, esp. 81 ff, 91 ff, 153 ff
Bhagavadgītā, Hill ... 10, 57, 82, 90, 93
Bhāradvāja Saṁhitā 190
Bible ... ... 46, 157 ff
Brahma Sūtras ... ... 60, 83 ff
Brāhmaṇa—
—Aitareya, Haug ... 3, 11, 16 ff, 78, 109
—Jaiminîya Upanishad 33, 46, 78
—Kaushîtaki 36, 64, 79
—Pañchaviṁśa 16
—Satapatha, Eggeling, 3 ff, 33, 48, 78, 109 ff, 147, 159, 175
—Taittirîya 33, 78
—Vaṁśa 180
Brāhmaṇa gītā 60
Bṛihaddevatā 36
Bṛihajjātaka, Varāhamihira 120
Bṛihat Saṁhitā 63, 174, 176, 179
Buddhacharita, Aśvaghosha ... 3 ff, 69, 125, 161
Buddhist India, Rhys Davids, Dr. T. W. 24, 67, 125, 147, 176

Cambridge History of India ... 87, 131
Catalogue of the Coins of the Andhra Dynasty 18
Catalogue of Indian (Gupta) Coins, Allan 150, 168 ff
Ceylonese Chronicles 55
—Mahāvaṁsa, Ed. and trans. Geiger 64
Chārudatta 86

PAGE

Chilappathikāram 181
Coins of Ancient India, Cunningham ... 106, 147, 176
Comparative Studies in Vaishnavism and Christianity, Dr. Seal ... ... 61, 92, 98, 134 ff
Corpus Inscriptionum Indicarum, Fleet ... 3, 90, 94, 165 ff

Dialogues of the Buddha, Rhys Davids, Dr. T. W. 24, 36, 95
Dictionary, Twentieth Century, Chambers 1
Divya Prabandham 182
Dynasties of the Kali Age, Pargiter ... 63, 150

Early History of India, Smith, V. A. 24, 39, 59, 70, 120, 150, 160
Early History of the Dekkan, Bhandarkar, Sir R. G. 24, 53
Encyclopaedia of Religion and Ethics ... 152
Epigraphia Indica ... 3, 22 f, 96, 99, 116, 162 ff
Essays, Miscellaneous, Colebrooke ... 4, 21
Ethics of India, Hopkins 155

Footfalls of Indian History, Niveditā ... 177

Gîtārthasaṁgraha, Yāmunāchārya ... 92, 192
Gospels ... ... 153 ff
Great Epic of India, Hopkins, 24, 46, 51, 54, 59, 68, 70, 101, 138, 154

Harigîtā 22, 91
Harivaṁśa ... 65, 69, 71, 73, 85, 88, 125, 143, 149 ff
Harshacharita, Bāṇa 3, 179
Heart of Hinduism, Radhakrishnan ... 36
Heart of Jainism, Mrs. Stevenson ... 65

PAGE

Hindu Gods and Heroes, Barnett ... 13, 111
Hinduism and Buddhism, Eliot ... 149, 151, 160
History of Indian Literature, Weber 16, 25, 45, 52, 62, 101, 150
History of Indian Literature, Winternitz... 69, 151
Hymns of the Āḷvārs 182

Index, Vedic Macdonell and Keith ... See Vedic Index
—Of names in the Mahābhārata, Sorrensen 4
Indian Antiquary ... ... 3 ff *passim*
Indian Culture 28
Indian Historical Quarterly ... 7, 30, 104, 117, 182 ff
Indian Philosophy, Max Müller ... 83 ff
Indian Philosophy, Radhakrishnan ... 36
Indians in Armenia 23
Indien und das Christentum ... 134
Indische Alterthums kunde ... 133
Indian Theism, Macnicol 18 ff, 41 ff, 60, 84, 91, 123, 127, 139, 155 ff, 192 ff
Indika, Megasthenes 4, 65, 67, 72
Indo-Aryan Races, Chanda 50
Introduction to the Bhagavadgītā, Garbe 85 ff, 91, 140, 159
Introduction to the Pañcarātra, Schrader 7, 31, 98, 122, 190
Introduction to the Ṛigveda Saṁhitā, Wilson ... ... 11 f
Introductory Essay to the Bhagavadgîtā, Telang ... ... 84 ff, 135 ff, 151

Jaimini Bhārata 143, 145
Jātakas—Ed. Cowell 3
—Dasabrāhmaṇa 43, 75
—Dasaratha 33

PAGE

—Dhūmakāri 75
—Ghata ... 4, 33, 38, 52, 60, 64 f, 72, 123, 162
—Kuṇāla 75
—Kurudhamma 43, 75
—Mahāummagga 172

Journal—
—Asiatic Society of Bengal ... 104
—Royal Asiatic Society of Great Britain ... ... 3 ff *passim*
—Vienna Oriental 3, 20

Kādambarî, Bāṇa 3, 84
Kalpas 27
Kāsikā 101
Kathāsaritsāgara 26
Kāvya-Mīmāṁsā 27
Kṛishṇa Charitra 178
Kumārasambhava 85

Life in Ancient India, P. T. S. Iyenger ... 36
Life of Madhva 77
List of Brāhmī Inscriptions, Lüders ... 22 ff, 116, 161 ff

Mahābhārata, Ed. P. Tarkaratna, Trans. by P. C. Roy and M. N. Dutt ... 3 ff *passim*
Māhābhāshya—Patañjali, Ed. Kielhorn 3 ff, 24, 37, 42, 48 f, 65, 67, 72 f, 87, 101, 104 ff, 131, 149, 176
Mahāpurusha-nirṇaya, Yāmunāchārya ... 192
Mahāvaṁsa, Geiger 64
Mahāyāna Sraddhotpāda 124, 161
Mahenjo-daro and Indus Culture, Marshall 148

PAGE

Mattavilāsa Prahasana 77
Memoirs of the Archæological Survey of India 22, 33, 70, 147, 161
Metrical Translations, Muir 133
Milinda-pañho 55
Modern Review 45
Mudrārākshasa 29
Mukundamālā 71
Mythologie, Polier 129

Nālâyira Prabandham 182
Nārāyaṇîya ... ... 21, 97 ff, 116, 134 ff, 175 ff
New Testament ... ... 153 ff
Niddesa 95
Nikāya, Aṅguttara 95
—Majjhima 96
Nirukta 3, 12, 69
Nyāya Tattva, Nāthamuni 20, 189
Nyāya Siddhāñjana, Srî Vedāntadeśika ... 189

Opinions, Poussin 127
Original Sanskrit Texts, Muir ... 11 ff, 128

Padāvalîs of Mediaeval Bengal ... 2
Pādmatantra 21, 35
Pancharātra Saṁhitās 98, 179, 190
Pāṇini, His Place in Sanskrit Literature, Goldstücker ... ... 25 ff
Periplus of the Erythræan Sea, Schoff ... 151
Philosophy of Ancient India, Garbe ... 61
Political History of Ancient India ... 104

Purāṇa—
—Agni 70, 150

PAGE

—Bhāgavata 3, 20, 39, 63, 70, 77, 143, 150, 175, 178, 181
—Bhavishyat 150
—Brahma 8, 44
—Brahmāṇḍa 63
—Brahmavaivartta 178
—Bṛihannāradîya 70
—Matsya 3, 44, 63, 72, 150, 175, 178
—Mārkaṇḍeya 70, 150
—Skanda 70, 150
—Vāyu ... ... 3, 63, 70, 72, 150 ff, 178
—Vishṇu 3, 50, 63, 98, 123, 143, 178

Raghuvaṁśa, Kālidāsa 29, 174
Rājataraṅginî 63, 179
Rāmacharitamānasa, Tulasîdāsa ... 2
Rāmānujanūrrandhādhi, Amudan ... 186
Rāmāyaṇa 77, 145
Religion and Philosophy of the Veda, Keith 12, 76

Religions of India—
—Barth ... ... 32, 40 ff, 52, 121, 160
—Hopkins, 11 ff, 38, 41 ff, 47, 73, 75, 79, 137, 144 ff, 155

Report of the Archæological Survey, Western India 151

Revelation 155

Sabdakalpadruma, R. K. Dev ... 121, 176
Sacred Books of the East, Max Müller ... 52
Saddharmapuṇḍarîka 39, 55, 124, 160
Saṁhitā (Veda)—
—Black Yajus 27
—Kāṭhaka 62, 64

PAGE

—Ṛigveda, Ajmer edition and translations by M. N. Dutt, R. C. Dutt and Wilson ... ... 3 ff, 11 ff *passim*
—Sāman 27
—Taittirîya 12, 33, 46, 78
—White Yajus 45

Sāṅdilya Sūtram 10
Saṅkara's Commentaries 3, 80, 86, 179
Saṅkara Vijaya 70
Sāṅkhyakārikā 91
Sanskrit Drama, Keith 49
Sanskrit Literature, Macdonell ... 24, 51, 66, 146
Sapta Satakam 172
Satasāhasrīsaṁhitā 69
Siddhitraya, Yāmunāchārya ... ... 20, 192 ff
Si-yu-ki, Hiuen Tsang 55
Songs of the Ālvārs ... ... 2, 20, 182 ff
Srī-bhāshya 188
Srī Rāmānujāchārya, S. K. Aiyangar ... 19, 182 ff
Srī Saṅkarāchārya, C. N. K. Aiyar ... 1, 65, 77
Sthavirāvalīcharita, Jacobi 121
Stotraratna, Yāmunāchārya 192
Studies in Indian Antiquities ... 69, 104, 125
Studies in Tamil Literature and History ... 182 ff
Sutta—Ambaṭṭha 36
—Dhammachakkappavattana ... 55, 91

Sūtra—
—Āpastamba, Ed. Dr. Bühler ... 2, 86, 131
—Bādarāyaṇa 3, 83
—Bodhāyana ... 3, 47 f, 74, 102, 106, 110 ff, 147 ff, 176
—Jaina ... ... 3, 64 f, 123
—Aupapātika 121
—Kalpa, Jacobi 67

PAGE

—Ṛishimaṇḍala 67
—Uttarūdhyayana ... 4, 34, 52, 65, 67, 72, 121
—Vaikhānasa 120

Tamils Eighteen Hundred Years Ago, Kanakasabhai 74, 152, 181
Tantras 107
Theism in Mediæval India 104, 160
Theragāthā 159
Tiruvāymoḻi ... ... 184 ff
Trikāṇḍaśesha 176
Trishashṭiśalākā-purusha-charita, Hemachandra 121

Upāṅga 121
Upanishad—
—Aitareya 66
—Bṛihadāraṇyaka 66, 84
—Chhāndogya 3, 7, 39, 51 ff, 60, 64 ff, 71 f, 78 f, 84, 89 122 ff, 146, 158 ff
—Kaṭha 3, 14, 84
—Kaushītaki 66
—Muṇḍaka 157
—Nṛisiṁhatāpanîya 84
—Śvetāśvatara 3, 84, 159
—Taittirîya 66

Vaikhānasa Dharma Sūtra 120
Vaishnavite Reformers of India, Rājagopālāchāriar. T. ... ... 20, 91, 182 ff
Vaiṣṇavism, Śaivism and Minor Religious Systems, Bhandarkar, Sir R. G. 37, 71 ff, 93 ff, 98, 115 139, 182 ff

	Page
Vajra-sūchî	69
Vārttikas, on Pāṇini's Grammar, Kātyāyana	25 ff
Vedānta, Teachings of, according to Rāmānuja, Sukhtankar, V. A. ...	20
Vedārtha Saṁgraha, Rāmānuja ...	20
Vedic Index	4, 47, 52, 148
Vishvaksena Saṁhitā	31, 175
Vedic Mythology, Macdonell ...	90, 140, 159
Vinaya Texts	149

GENERAL INDEX [1]

PAGE

Abhinavagupta 70
Ābhira ... ...74, 144, 151 f.
Achchhāvāka 17
Achaemenian conquest 29
Āchārya, Tamil ... ... 2 ff., 20, 31, 188 ff.
Achyuta 57
Actors of Mathurâ 164
Aditi 40
Āditya ... 11, 16, 82, 110 f., 157 ff., 172
Adonis 41
Advaita (Philosophy) 194
Agastya 33
Ahiṁsā ... ... 7, 81, 89, 123 f.
Aihole Inscription 62
Aiyar, C. N. Krishna Swami 1, 65, 77
Aiyangar, S. K. ... ...3, 19, 182 ff.
Ājīvikas ... ... 95, 119 f.
Ājīvikism 6
Akki-Alwan (court poet of the Chola king) 191
Alagarkoil 183
Ālavandār (Victor), see Yūmunāchārya
Alexander 193
Alexandria 134, 136
Allahabad praśasti 47, 181
Allan ... ... 150, 168 ff.
Āḷvār ... ... 2, 20, 31 ff., 180 ff.

[1] The references are not exhaustive. The attention of the reader is invited to the Preface.

PAGE

Amudan (author) 186
Aṁsumatî 36
Aṁtalikita (see Antialkidas).
Ānakadundubhi 72
Ānandagiri 70
Ananta (The Serpent)... ... ... 164, 171
Anantasvāmin (a name of Vishṇu) ... 161, 169
Āṇḍāl (the 9th Āḷvār, a woman) 182, 184
Āṅgirasa, Ghora ... 51 ff., 64, 73, 79 ff., 122, 157
Āṅgirasa, Kṛishṇa 36
Aniruddha 98, 175
Antialkidas (Indo-Greek king) ... 22, 28, 99, 131
Antiochos 28
Āpastamba 2, 86, 131
Apollo 129
Arishṭanemi (a Jaina Tīrthaṅkara) ... 64, 121
Arjuna 22, 24, 31, 35, 45, 76, 85, 91, 101, 112, 162, 175
Arjunakas 24, 95
Armenia 23
Āryya-Sātvata-Yogāchāryya 94, 165, 172
Asia Minor 144
Aśoka ... ...6, 39, 55, 95 f., 103, 107
Assyria 29
Āśvalāyana 54, 68
Aśvamedha 96, 117, 132
Athene 147
Aurṇavābha 12, 128
Avantivarman 179
Avatāra (doctrine of) ... ... 9, 13, 109, 124, 141, 154, 158 f., 173 ff., 183
Avidyā (doctrine of) 192
Ayodhyā 128

PAGE

Bacchus 105
Badami, bas relief 70, 147, 151, 180
Badari 114
Baladeva, Balarāma. (See also Saṅkarshaṇa.) ... ... 40, 73, 106, 121, 147, 162 ff., 181
Baladevavatikā 95
Baladevas 121
Bali (mythical king) 105, 169, 174
Balibandha 105
Baukimchandra (Bengali writer) 3, 178
Besnagar ... ... 13, 22, 28, 32, 89, 93, 99 ff., 102, 110, 116, 131
Bhadrabāhu 67
Bhāgavata, Paramabhāgavata ... 21 ff., 30, 35, 94 ff., 99, 116, 120, 131, 168, 171, 179 ff.
Bhāgavatism ... ... 5 ff., 21 ff., 30, 89 ff., 102 ff., 119 ff., 161 ff., 180 ff.
Bhakti ... ...10, 18 ff., 30, 93, 139 f., 159, 167, 194
Bhaktimārga 139, 152
Bhanḍarkar, Dr. D. R. 120, 166
Bharahat Tope, see Bharhut.
Bhārata war ... ... 62 ff.
Bhārgava, Rāma 175
Bharhut 147, 160, 176
Bhaṭṭāchārya, Vidhuśekhara 104
Bhāsa 86
Bhīmasena, Bhīma ... ... 43 f., 162
Bhīshmastavarāja 80, 82, 108
Bhitarī Pillar Inscription ... 72, 146, 168
Bhojas 57

PAGE

Bhūdevī 177
Bhūtattar (2nd Āḷvār) ... ... 182 f., 187
Boar Incarnation ... ... 159, 170, 173 ff.
Böhtlingk ... ... 24 f.
Bṛindāban, Vṛindāvana 40, 148
Buddha, Śākya sage ... 1, 39, 42, 55, 60, 77 f., 96, 124 ff., 132, 141, 149, 160, 175
Buddhism ... ... 6 f., 54, 68, 96, 123
Budha Gupta 170

Caldwell, Bishop 185
Chaitanya 2
Chakrabhṛit (Kṛishṇa-Vishṇu) 169
Chakrapālita 169
Chakrasvāmin (Kṛishṇa-Vishṇu) 166
Chandra, king ... ... 6, 165 f.
Chandra Gupta I (Gupta king) 150
Chandra Gupta II, Vikramāditya 168
Chandravarman 166
Chhagalaga 168
China Inscription ... ... 161 f., 180
Chitrakūṭa svāmin 169
Choraśāstra 77
Christ, Jesus ... ... 128 ff.
Christianity ... ... 6, 19, 128 ff., 193
Christophoros 143
Cosmas Indicopleustes 149, 160

Dadhikarṇa 164
Dahrasena 18, 167
Dakshiṇāpatha 117
Dama, tyāga, apramāda ... 13, 88, 93, 100, 103, 155
Dāmodara 42, 48, 74, 148

PAGE

Dāśarathi (Rāma) ... ... 10, 31, 146, 174 f., 184
Denarius 70
Deogarh temple ... ... 171 f.
Deussen 92
Devadhammikas 95
Devakî 40, 56, 72, 78, 130, 146, 169
Devakîputra ... ... 51 f., 56 ff., 61, 77
Devî (the title of the royal consorts of the Gupta Emperors) 177
Dhamma 116
Dhanañjaya 43
Dhanyavishṇu 170
Dharasena II 171
Dharma ... ... 113 f.
Dhṛitarāshṭra Vaichitravîrya 40, 62
Dhruvasena I 171
Dīkshā 16, 79
Dionysos, Greek God ... ... 41 f.
Diya (Dion) 99
Draviḍa 181
Draupadî 45
Duḥśalā 143
Durvasas 129
Duryodhana 75, 97
Dvaipāyana 33
Dvita ... ... 132 f.
Dwārakā 41

Ekadaṇḍin 120
Egypt, Egyptian 41, 134
Ekānaṁsā 176
Ekāntika 21, 91
Ekata ... ... 132 f.

	Page
Elūra	146
Eraṇ Stone Pillar Inscription	169 f.
Eucharist	135
Fish, Avatāra	174 f.
Gadhwā Inscription	169
Gandhāra	29, 95
Gājāyana	96
Gaṅgdhāra Inscription	167
Garuḍa, Garuḍadhvaja ...	22, 90, 99, 102, 110, 170
Gautama (Buddha), see Buddha.	
Gayā peak	12, 128
Ghata (Bodhisatva)	38, 64, 123
Ghora (Āṅgirasa)	51 ff., 73, 79 ff., 89, 93, 122, 157
Ghosuṇḍî Inscription ...	23, 32, 96 ff., 109, 117, 131
Gītā and the Gospels	153 ff.
Gītā and the Mandasor Record	173
Gīta, date of	84 ff., 154
Gnostics	135
Gobala Vārshṇa	46, 78
God as lover	184
Gopā	11, 47, 55, 74, 111, 148
Gopāla	46
Gopendra	46
Gopī	53, 73
Gopījanavallabha	53
Gospels	129, 153, 158
Gotamaka	24, 95
Govinda	41, 46, 74, 148 f., 169
Granthikas	49 f.
Greek Goddesses	177, *cf.* 147
Greeks, see Yauna.	
Guptan Vaishṇavism	172 ff.

PAGE

Haṁsa Avatāra 175
Hardy 140
Hari 10, 112, 114, 132
Hārita, Kṛishṇa 36
Hāritī 148
Harivaṁśa, date of 69, 150
Harshavardhana, Harsha ... ... 84, 178 f.
Hebrew seers ... ... 139, *cf.* 195
Heliodora, Heliodoros (ambassador of the Indo-Greek king Antialkidas) 2, 22, 99 ff., 131, 155
Herakles ... ... 38, 75, 94, 101 f.
Here 147
Hiraṇyagarbha 139
Holtzmann 92
Hṛishīkeça 137
Hultzsch, Dr. 186
Huns 6, 170

Ida (Indra), see also Indra 116
Ikshvāku 90
Indo-China 151
Indra ... ... 14 ff., 76, 113, 156, 167
Indradatta 167
Indrota 180
Issykul (Lake) 134
Īśvara Bhatta 191

Jackson 151
Jaina, Jainism 6, 95, 121, 179
Jāmbavatī 165, 172
Janaka 125
Janamejaya 22, 180
Janārdana ... ... 98, 105, 164, 170, 172 f.
Janmāshṭamī 130, 142, 145

	Page
Jarāsandha	75
Jaṭilā	44
Jaṭilakas	95
Jayanātha (king)	171
Jayaswāl	12, 127, 148
Jesus, see Christ.	
Jethrow	46
Jina, Tîrthaṅkara	1, 64 f., 121
Jishṇu	144
Jīva	97
Jobares (river), see Yamunā.	
Jñāna Yoga	92, 194
Juda	129
Jumna, see Yamunā.	
Junāgaḍh Inscription	169, 174
Kālakāchāryya	120
Kalhaṇa	63
Kālidāsa	29, 85, 174
Kāliya	129, 164
Kaliyuga Era	62 ff.
Kalki Avatāra	175
Kallar (caste)	185
Kāmboja	28, 68
Kaṁsa	36 f., 48ff., 74f., 143, 145, 149
Kaṁsabhaktā	48, 51
Kaṁsabadha	105
Kāñchî	181, 183, 186
Kaṇha, see Kṛishṇa.	
Kaṇha (seer)	36
Kaṇha dîpāyana	33, 121
Kanishka	125
Kapila	39, 59, 67, 91, 132, 175

	Page
Kashmere, Kaśmîra	138, 179
Karikal	181
Karmakāṇḍa, Karmamārga	9, 193
Kāsiputa Bhāgabhadra	99 f.
Kauravya, Koravya	43
Kavîra	2, 31, 196
Kāviripaddinam	181
Kennedy	134, 146
Kern	119 ff.
Keśava	106, 118, 120, 162
Khoh Copper-plate Inscription of Sarvanātha	69, 85, 150, 171
Kielhorn	37
Kîkaṭa	77
Kleisobora	38, 94
Kleuker	129
Kṛishṇa Vāsudeva—	
ignorance about	1
true character	5, 32 ff.
incarnation of Vishṇu	10
Kṛishṇa cult in Armenia	23
fountain head of Vaishṇavism	31
identity with Vāsudeva	36 ff.
not a solar deity	42
not a patron god of a wild tribe ...	43
not a vegetation deity	46
his human character	51 ff., 102
his life and teachings	62 ff.
his apotheosis	100
connection with solar worship	89 ff., 102
identification with Nārāyaṇa-Vishṇu	106 ff., 118
regarded as a great personage by Jainas and Buddhists	121, 124

	Page
hostility towards him	76, 108
Krishṇa and Christ	128 ff.
festival of the birth-day	142 ff.
pastoral associations ...	46 f., 55, 73 f., 148
connection with Ābhīras ...	74, 144, 151
epigraphic references ...	22 f., 96 ff., 161 ff.
Krishṇa worship in the Far South of India	181 ff.
Krishṇapura	38
Kritamālā	181
Kubjā	143
Kulaśekhara	71, 182, 184
Kuntī	127
Kuru	35, 43 ff., 75
Kurukshetra	62, 64
Kushān	6, 125, 163 f.
Kuvera	117
Lakshmî	168 ff., 176 f.
Logos	135
Lokapālas	117
Maṇḍana Miśra	194
Madhva, Vaishnava Reformer	77, 86, 195
Madhurā, Upper, see also Mathurā ...	33, 72
Madhurakavi, Āḷvār	182, 184
Madhusūdana	167
Madonna	142, 147, 158
Madurā (in the Far South)	181
Magaṇḍikas	95
Magadha	75, 94, 165, 168
Mahābalipuram	187
Mahābhārata, date of	67 f.
Mahāpadma Nanda	25, 63

PAGE
Mahāpurusha (Great Person) 137
Mahāvīra 1, 6, 67, 119, 123
Mahāvishṇu 184
Mahenjo Daro 148
Mahomed 55
Makaradhvaja 23
Makkhali Gosāla, teacher of the Ājīvika sect 119
Māliyā Copper-plate Inscription 171
Mallinātha 85
Mandasor Inscription ... ... 166 f., 173
Mandor Sculptures 151
Maṅgaleśa 180
Manichaeans 128
Mannargudi 188, 191
Manu 90
Manu (self-born) 114
Mārtāṇḍa 40
Mary, the Virgin 142, 146
Mātṛivishṇu, Mahārāja 170
Mathurā ... ...5, 33, 38, 72, 94, 96, 143, 145, 163 f., 176, 190
Mauryas 6
Max Müller 52, 83, 86
Mayūrākshaka 167
Majumdar, N. G. 163
Media 29
Megasthenes, the Greek ambassador at the court of Chandra Gupta Maurya 4, 38, 65, 67, 72, 94, 101, 163
Meherauli Iron pillar 166
Methora, see Mathura.
Meru, Mount 135

	Page
Mîrā Bāī	184
Mihiragula	178
Mīmāṁsā philosophers	193 f.
Mitra coin	106
Monism	194
Mora Inscription	32, 161
Moses	46, 55
Muradvish	171
Nāga Statuette Inscription	164
Nāgas	113, 164
Nammāḷvār	182 ff.
Nanda, foster father of Kṛishṇa ...	40, 119, 143, 145
Nanda, king of Magadha. See Mahāpadma.	
Nanda Vaccha, religious teacher ...	119
Nānāghāṭ Inscription	23, 116 ff.
Ṇandibala	164
Nara (Arjuna)	31, 112 ff., 175
Nārada	121, 133 ff.
Narasiṁha	171, 174 f.
Narasiṁhavarman I, king of Kāñchī ...	187
Naravarman	166
Nārāyaṇa ...	6, 32, 111 ff., 115 f., 120, 132 ff., 170, 173, 177, 181, 183
Nārāyaṇa distinguished from the Ādityas	111, 112
Nārāyaṇa, solar associations	115 f.
Nārāyaṇavāṭa	96, 109
Nāsik Cave Inscription	161 f.
Nāthamuni, Tamil Āchārya ...	20, 183, 188 ff.
Ṇeminātha	64

PAGE

Nestorian Missions 145, 152
New Testament 153
Nigaṇṭhas (Jainas) 95
Niyoga 44
Northern Kurus 45
Nṛisiṁha 175

Osiris 41

Pallas, the Greek goddess 177
Pallava Parameśvara 186
Pāñchāla 44, 106
Pāñcharātra ... 21, 97, 112, 122, 179, 192
Paṇḍaia 75
Pāṇḍava ... 35, 41, 43 ff., 75, 130, 162
Pāṇḍya 152, 184
Pāṇini, date of ... ... 24 ff.
Paramabhāgavata 116, 168
Parameśvara Vinnagara 186
Parameśvara Varman II 186
Pārāśarī 96
Paribbājakas, wandering ascetics ... 95, 121
Parikshit ... ... 63 f.
Parivrājaka Kings 170
Pārśvanātha, the 23rd Jaina Tīrthaṅkara—immediate predecessor of Mahāvīra ... 65, 132
Parthia, (Parthians Pahlavas) 68, 134, 138
Pārvatī 176
Patañjali ... 24, 36 ff., 48 ff., 65 ff., 104 ff., 151, 158
Pāṭaliputra 25, 27
Pathārī Sculptures 147, 171

PAGE

Pauṇḍra Vāsudeva 34
Periy Āḷvār 182, 184
Peter 129
Pey Āḷvār ... ... 182 f.
Pillar Edict 95, 103
Piper 146
Pishṭapurî 171
Polier 129
Poussin 127
Poygai, the first Āḷvār ... ... 182 f.
Prabhākara 194
Pradyumna 23, 98, 175
Prakṛiti 9, 98, 177
Prakaṭāditya 171
Prapatti, Doctrine of ... 189 f., 196, *cf.* 167
Prasāda 2, 10, 18
Prati-Vāsudevas 121
Prayer in Hindu worship 140
Puṇḍarīkāksha, Āchārya 190
Purāṇas, date of 70, 150, 177
Purusha ... ... 9, 111, 166, 172 f., 177
Purusha Yajña ... ... 79 f.
Purushottama 10
Pushyamitras 169
Pūrva Mīmāṁsā 9, 194
Pushkaraṇa 166

Rādhā 172
Rājuvula—coins of 147
Mahākshatrapa of Mathurā ... 32, 161
Rāma (Balarāma), see Baladeva.
Rāma, Bhārgava 175
Rāma, Dāśarathi ... ... 10, 31, 146, 174 f.
Rāmamiśra, Āchārya 191

PAGE

Rāmānanda, Vaishṇava teacher 31, 174, 196
Rāmānuja ... 2 ff., 6, 9, 19 f., 31, 86, 185 ff., 193
Rāmanavamî 145
Rāma worship 174
Raṅganātha 185
Rao Gopînāth 185, 187
Ṛishabha 175
Ṛita 13, 140
Rock Edicts of Aśoka 28, 55
Rohiṇeyya 38
Rohiṇî 147
Romakas (the Romans) 68
Rudra ... ... 110 f., 164

Śaka ... ... 6, 30, 45, 163 f.
Śakakāla 63
Śākapūṇi 12, 128
Śākya, see Buddha.
Śākyasiṁha, see also Buddha 66
Śalākāpurusha 121
Saṁkshoba, Parivrājaka mahārāja ... 170
Sāṁkhya 67, 69, 98, 177
Samudragupta 47, 173, 181
Sanakānika 168
Śāṇḍilya ... ... 10, 179 f.
Sāndīpani 73
Śaṅkarāchārya ... 9, 86, 153, 179, 192, 194 f.
Saṅkarshaṇa, see also Baladeva 9, 23, 35, 73, 95 ff., 105 ff., 116 f., 122, 162, 175
Śārṅgin 168
Sāriputta, a disciple of Buddha 124
Sārnāth Stone Inscription 171

	Page
Śārvanātha, see also Khoh Copper-plate Inscription ...	171
Sarvatāta	96, 100, 132, 165
Śāstrî, Haraprasad, M.M.	166 ff.
Satagopa, Satakopa—the fifth Āḷvār. See "Nammāḷvār" ...	20, 182 ff.
Sati Sirimata	117
Sātvata	21, 35, 38, 57, 65, 72, 77 f., 89 f., 94, 122, 165, 172, 192
Sauri—Kṛishṇa	125
Schroeder, Von	52
Sea of Milk	114, 135, 137
Senart	42, 127
Seven Divine Mothers	146
Serpent worship	163 f.
Śipivishṭa	13, 48, 111
Sirimā Devatā, see Śrî.	
Śiva-worshippers	2, 76, 164
Skanda Gupta	72, 168 f.
Socrates	65
Soḍāsa	72, 161 f.
Solar worship ...	...5, 57, 80, 89 ff., 102, 172
Sourasenoi	38, 72, 94, 102
Śraddhā	139, 154, 158
Śrī, Lakshmī	147, 173, 176 f.
Śrīraṅgam	183 ff.
Śrī Vaishṇava	3, 190, 193 ff.
Śrî Vedānta Deśika, a Vaishṇava teacher of the school of Rāmānuja ...	189, 192
Śrī Yajña Śātakarṇi	162, 180
St. Chrysostom	153
Sten Konow	151
Strauss, Dr.	158

PAGE

St. Thomas 160
Subandhu 150
Subhadrā, Kṛishṇa's sister 176, 180
Sūris 13, 21
Suśuniā Inscription of Chandravarman 166
Suzuki, Teitaro ... ... 124 ff.
Svāmin, Govindāchārya 35
Śvetadvīpa, the White Island ... ...114 f., 130 ff.
Syria, Syrian 23, 135, 144

Takakusu 152
Tamil Vaishṇavism ... ... 19 f., 180 ff.
Tāmraparṇī 181, 184
Tedaṇḍika 95
Tīrthakara, Tīrthaṅkara 64, 121, 175
Tiru(j)ñāna Sambandar, a Śaiva saint ... 186
Tirukkoilur, a city 183
Tirukkotiyūr Nambi, a teacher of Rāmānuja 186
Tirumaliśai, the fourth Āḷvār ... ... 182 f.
Tirumaṅgai, the twelfth Āḷvār ... ... 182, 185 f.
Tirupati 183
Tiruppāṇ, the eleventh Āḷvār 182, 185
Tiruvallari 190
Tiruvāymoli 184
Toṇḍaraḍippoḍi, the tenth Āḷvār ... ... 182, 184 f.
Toramāṇa 170
Traikūṭaka 18, 167
Tridaśa 167
Trita ... ... 132 f.
Trivikrama, see also Vāmana 183
Tukārāma 2
Tulasī Dāsa 2, 196

PAGE

Tumain, carvings at 163
Tusām Rock Inscription 116, 165
Udaygiri Cave Inscription 168
Upasada 79
Upasāgara 72
Urukrama 4
Utgikar 84, 91, 140, 159
Utpala ... ... 63, 119 f.
Uttarāpatha 28
Uyyakkondar, the surname given to Puṇḍarīkāksha by his guru Nāthamuni 190

Vayiramega 187
Vaishṇava ... ... 17 f., 167
Vaishṇavī 173, 177
Vaishṇavism ... ...1 ff., 5, 8, 10 ff., 31, 172
Valabhī 171
Vāmana (Dwarf Avatāra) ... 13, 48, 55, 148, 160, 174 f.
Vaṅga 166
Varāhī 146
Vardhamāṇa, see Mahāvīra.
Vārkshī 44
Varsha 25
Vārttikas of Kātyāyana ... ... 25 f.
Varuṇa ... ... 16, 18, 31, 117, 139 f., 159
Vāsava 117
Vasus 112
Vasu, Uparichara 132
Vasudeva 5, 72
Vāsudeva, meaning of ... ... 34 f.

PAGE

Vāsudeva, the Sātvata prince. See Kṛishṇa Vāsudeva.
Vāsudeva, the king of the Puṇḍras ... 34
Vāsudevas 121
Vāsudevaka ... ... 23 f., 95, 180
Vāsudeva-bhaktāḥ 48, 51
Vāsudevavargyaḥ, Vāsudevavarginaḥ ... 104
Vātāpi 33
Vedisiri 117
Vidhi Yajña 7, 80, 93
Vibhavas 175
Vīranārāyaṇapura 188, 191
Viśishṭādvaita School of Philosophy ... 189, 191, 193
Vishṇu ... ... 6 f., 10 ff., 32, 86, 106, 108 ff., 165, 168 ff., 172
Vishṇuchitta 182, 184
Vishṇu gopa 47, 149, 181
Vishṇupada (Gayā) 12, 128
Vishṇupada, heaven 14, 115
Vishṇupada (in Upper India) 166
Viśvakāya 36
Viśvavarman 167
Vivasvān... 90
Vṛindābana. See Brindaban.
Vṛishṇi ... ... 5, 32 f., 65, 72, 77 f., 89, 162
Vṛitra 15
Vyūha 9, 97, 175

White Island, see Śvetadvīpa.

Yaçodā, Yaśodā 40, 143, 147
Yādava 35, 40, 72, 89, 93
Yājñavalkya 26

PAGE

Yajña (sacrifice) identified with Vishṇu 15
Yamunā (Jumna) 5, 40, 46, 94, 190
Yāmunāchārya ... ... 20, 92, 191 ff.
Yāska 69, 127
Yaśodharman 178
Yātrās 105
Yauna, Yavana ... ... 28 f.
Yoga and Bhakti 166, 172
Yoga Sūtras 139
Yuddhiṭṭhila, Yudhishṭhira 43, 129

Zenob 23

BY THE SAME AUTHOR

I.—Political History of Ancient India

From the Accession of Parikshit to the Extinction of the Gupta Dynasty

Third Edition

Royal 8vo. Pp. xix, 469. Price Rs. 7-8

Published by the Calcutta University

THE HINDUSTHAN REVIEW.—It is learned and luminous and is a scientific treatise based on the results of research into the records and materials of ancient Indian history, of which it is a sound and an accurate digest, interestingly put together. It is about the best text-book of the subject it deals with.

Some opinions on the earlier editions and on Part I :—

DR. L. D. BARNETT, LONDON.—The author treats his materials with a certain degree of originality, but at the same time he preserves throughout a well-balanced judgment and never sacrifices critical caution to the passion for novel theories.........This interesting book......shews judgment, ingenuity, and learning. And not the least of the author's merits is that he can write plain English.

PROFESSOR HULTZSCH, HALLE, GERMANY.—Your valuable work......is the outcome of extensive researches and throws much light on the darkest and most debated periods of Indian history. You have succeeded in building up an intelligible account from the stray and imperfect materials which are available to the historian of those times.

PROFESSOR JOLLY, WURZBURG, GERMANY.—Many thanks for your splendid volume.........What an enormous mass of evidence has been collected and discussed in this work, an important feature of which is the quotation of the original texts along with their translation which makes it easy to control the conclusions arrived at. The ancient geography, not less than the ancient history of India, has been greatly furthered by your researches and much new light has been thrown on some of the most vexed problems of Indian Archaeology and Chronology. The indices are very copious and the study of your work is greatly facilitated by them.

PROFESSOR PELLIOT, PARIS.—Le nom de I'auteur est garant du serieux du travail.

PROFESSOR JARL CHARPENTIER, UPSALA, SWEDEN.—Professor Ray Chaudhuri belongs to a set of young Hindu scholars who, combining the traditional education of a Pandit with a thorough training in English. German or French Universities, have lately been carrying on deep and fruitful researches in the various domains of Indian lore...... Even the student, who on essential points does differ widely from the opinions expressed by Professor Ray Chaudhuri, must willingly recognize his high merits as a scholar.

PROFESSOR A. SCHEPOTIEFF, UFA, RUSSIA.—For our study of the history of the Ancient Age your Political History of Ancient India is of very great importance (trans. from original).

C. E. A. W. OLDHAM (J. R. A. S.)—Part I of Professor Ray Chaudhuri's work deals with the period from Parikṣhit to Bimbisāra. The author seeks to show, as he tells us in his preface, "that chronological relation of the national transactions before 600 B.C. is not impossible." He has laid under contribution the usual authorities, the Vedic, Puranic, Buddhist, and Jaina texts—though he does not appear to place much reliance upon the last-named (*cf.* pp. 6 and 72). A vast mass of records has been collated, and the evidence marshalled in a very concise and able, and in some respects original, manner. The apposite quotations from the original texts are useful. Professor Ray Chaudhuri regards Parikṣit I and Parikṣit II, as they are named by the late Mr. Pargiter in his *Ancient Indian Historical Tradition*, as being probably one and the same king, and as identifiable with the Vedic Parikṣit. By "the great Janaka" he refers to the Janaka of the later Vedic texts, whose court is said to have been thronged with Brāhmaṇas, and not to the traditional first king Janaka, the eponymous founder of the Janakavaṁśa, or to Janaka Sīradhvaja, the reputed father of Sītā, Synchronizing Guṇākhya Sāṅkhāyana with Āśvalāyana and the Buddha, he inclines, it seems, to place Parikṣit in the ninth, and the "great Janaka" in the seventh century B.C. though he wisely avoids coming to any positive conclusion as to these debatable dates, and points out that if the evidence of the Purāṇas were accepted we would have to place them some five centuries earlier. If it could be established that Parikṣit came into power at the beginning of the ninth century, or the end of the tenth, this would help to corroborate the approximate chronology suggested by Mr. Pargiter, having regard also to the synchronism between Senapati Bārhadratha and Adhisīmakṛṣṇa. But until more convincing evidence is discovered most scholars will probably agree in the verdict of Vincent Smith that nothing approaching exact chronology is yet available for periods anterior to about 650 B.C.

Much of the matter in Part II will perhaps be familiar to students of Indian history ; but it has been arranged in a fresh and scholarly manner, while several important suggestions have been made on different questions. One or two of these may be cited as examples. On pp. 72-3 reasons are set forth for accepting the Ceylon tradition that Śiśunāga was later than Bimbisāra. The view recorded by Mahāmahopādhāya (*sic*) H. P. Sāstrī that the ultimate dismemberment of the Mauryan empire was due to a reaction promoted by the Brāhmaṇas, is vigorously controverted. Whatever other causes may have operated, and Professor Ray Chaudhuri undoubtedly lays his finger on more than one such, Brahmanical influences cannot be ignored. The arguments used for holding that Demetrius,[1] rather than Menander, was the Yavana invader of the Madhyadeśa in the time of Pushyamitra, and that Simuka, the founder of the Sātavāhana dynasty, must be placed in the first century B.C., deserve careful consideration.

Since Hoernle made his well-known suggestion as to the identity of Devagupta, mentioned in two inscriptions of Harṣavardhana, several writers have attempted to frame the history of the later Guptas of Eastern Mālava and Bihār and the Maukharis of Kanauj. The period presents many difficulties, which are not likely to be solved until some further evidence reveals itself. Having regard to the conditions of the times and the bitter enmity of the Maukharis,

1 For the latest reading of the Hāthigumphā inscription reference t the Yavana king, see *JBORS*, XIII, 228.

who were then very powerful, it seems unlikely that the Susthitavarman mentioned in the Aphsaṇḍ (*sic*) inscription of Ādityasena as having been defeated by Mahāsenagupta of E. Mālava, could have been the king of Kāmarūpa, as the author states. Fleet's suggestion that he was the Maukhari king of that name,[1] whom we know to have been contemporaneous with Mahāsenagupta, seems more probable.

Not the least valuable part of the contents of this volume are the numerous comments on the geographical information supplied in the records quoted ; and it is a matter of regret that of the five maps entered in the table of Contents (p. xvi), only one, *viz.*, that of "Bhāratavarsha" appears in the volume before us. As regards this map we are not told what specific period, if any, it refers to. In any case, the positions assigned to the Niṣādas, S. Kosala, Kāmboja, and the Rikṣa mountains seem to call for some explanation. On the other hand, the geographical information given in the text is extensive, and often suggestive, and it indicates that much attention has been devoted to this important auxiliary to ancient Indian historical research. The indexes, both bibliographical and general, have been very well prepared.

PROFESSOR A. BERRIEDALE KEITH, EDINBURGH.—I have read through the work and find it to contain much that is valuable. The author has arrived at clearly cut opinions on many of the chief difficulties in the history of early India ; he has formulated them effectively, and as a result, even when they do not commend themselves as final solutions, they will serve to promote the discussion and to facilitate further fruitful research. He observes a due sense of proportion and is well read in the literature. The work accordingly may justly be deemed a most valuable contribution to the subject-matter of which it treats.

PROFESSOR WILH GEIGER, MUNCHEN-NEUBIBERG, GERMANY.—I highly appreciate Mr. Ray Chaudhuri's work as a most happy combination of sound scientific method and enormous knowledge of both Brahmanical and non-Brahmanical literature. The work is written in lucid style inspite of its intricate subject and affords a mass of valuable evidence, throwing much light on the whole period of Indian History dealt in it. I see with special pleasure and satisfaction that we now are enabled by the author's penetrating researches to start in Indian chronology from the 9th instead of the 6th or 5th century B.C.

[1] No Maukhari king of that name is known [H.C.R.C.].

K. P. Jayaswal, Patna.—I am very thankful to you (Raychaudhuri) for your valuable book. I am glad that you devote your attention to Hindu geography as well.

Professor Jackson, Columbia University, New York.—I can see the scholarly research which you have put into the volume, and am glad to have such a work for future reference in my historical studies.

Professor Louis de la Vallee Poussin, Brussels, Belgium.—I believe that the book is well designed and has the twofold merit of collecting a vast amount (and in some chapters, an exhaustive one) of references, and of giving a clear and reasonable *exposé* of the main line of this history. I agree with the author on several controverted points of chronology.

Mrs. C. A. F. Rhys Davids.—Dr. Chaudhuri has made debtors of us all.

S. M. Edwardes. (*The Indian Antiquary*, July, 1927, p. 140.)—Professor Raychaudhuri's book forms a solid contribution to the discussion of the various problems implicit in the early history of India.

Professor E. J. Rapson, Cambridge.—My best thanks for the kind present of a copy of the "Political History of Ancient India," which I am very glad to possess and which I shall find most useful for reference.

Professor Sten Konow, Norway.—The book is a very useful contribution.

Sitaram Kohli, Lahore.—I have immensely liked your book "Political History of Ancient India."

C. S. Srinivasachari, South India.—Our author rightly holds the balance between the views of Pargiter which would give excessive value to Kshatriya tradition whose date allowed of manipulation to serve dynastic ends and the value of Vedic tradition whose two strong points are its priority of date and freedom from textual corruption.

W. Charles de Silva, Colombo.—I have the greatest pleasure to express my high appreciation of your very valuable and learned article (Part I of the Political History).

Professor E. Washburn Hopkins.—It is a fine augury for Indian scholarship when native scholars of the first rank take seriously in hand the great problem of untangling the web of Indian history. To this work your book is a valuable contribution.

PROFESSOR H. JACOBI, BONN.—Very suggestive and contains some important details.

PROFESSOR F. OTTO SCHRADER.—I have read the book with increasing interest and do not hesitate to say that it contains a great many details which will be found useful by later historians. The portion I enjoyed most is that on the sixteen Mahājanapadas.

II. The Early History of the Vaishnava Sect

First Edition

Demy 8vo. Pp. xii, 146. Price Rs. 2-13

Published by the Calcutta University

OPINIONS AND REVIEWS

PROFESSOR E. WASHBURN HOPKINS, YALE UNIVERSITY, AMERICA.—Your book has given me great satisfaction...... I am particularly pleased to see an incisive study of this kind in the realm of religious history.........Believe me, in the hope of further contributions of this character from your able pen.........

PROFESSOR A. BERRIEDALE KEITH, EDINBURGH UNIVERSITY.—While I do not concur in your view as to the original character of Kṛṣṇa, I recognise the care with which you have investigated the issue, and value highly the elaborate collation of the evidence which your work contains, and which will render it of much service to all students of this doubtless insoluble problem. The stress laid on the epigraphic evidence and the full use made of it is of special value, while in many details your opinions are of interest and value, as in the case of the date of Pāṇini.........

SIR GEORGE GRIERSON.—Very interesting and informing.........The book is full of matter which is of great importance for the history of religion in India and will form a valued addition to my collection of books on the subject...

F. E. PARGITER, OXFORD.—I agree with you in discarding various theories, but I don't think Kṛṣṇa Devakīputra is the famous Kṛiṣṇa, and it seems to me your exposition can stand just as well without the identification as with it. Your book will help to elucidate the whole matter, but are you sure that the cult does not owe something to Christianity?

PROFESSOR F. OTTO SCHRADER, KIEL, GERMANY.—I perfectly agree with your opinion that the Chāndogya passage on Kṛṣṇa Devakīputra and his teaching is to be considered as the first historical record of Bhāgavatism. There were, of course, many Kṛṣṇas, but to conjecture that more than one was also a Devakīputra, is to my mind an unscientific boldness which is the less justifiable as the teachings mentioned in that passage, as you show, perfectly agree with those, *e.g.*, of the Bhagavad-gitā and Ṛk. quoted with the famous तद्विष्णो परमं पदं।.........

PROFESSOR GARBE, TUBINGEN, GERMANY.—I have read your book with the greatest interest and perfectly agree with you in the main points, as to the personality of Kṛṣṇa and the development of Bhāgavatism.........You have brought together much important material and elucidated the dark early history of Bhāgavatism as far as possible.

THE TIMES LITERARY SUPPLEMENT, MAY 12, 1921.—The lectures of Mr. Hemchandra Ray Chaudhuri on the early history of the Vaishṇava Sect read almost as would a Bampton lecture on the "Historical Christ" to a Christian audience. They are an attempt to disentangle the authentic figure of Krishna from the mass of Puranic legend and gross tradition, from the wild conjectures and mistaken, if reasoned, theories which surround his name. The worship of Krishna is not a superstitious idolatry ; it is the expression of the Bhakti, the devotional faith of an intellectual people, and many missionaries, ill-equipped for dealing with a dimly understood creed would do well to study this little volume.........

JOURNAL ASIATIQUE, JANUARY-MARCH, 1923, PARIS.—Dans le domaine historique, signalons un travail plein de merite de M. Hemchandra Ray Chaudhuri. *Materials for the Study of the Early History of the Vaishnava Sect.* (Dr. Jules Bloch of Paris.)

DR. JULES BLOCH, PARIS.—My Guru, Sylvain Lévi, who has come back from his travels, told me also of his esteem for that book.

JOURNAL OF THE ROYAL ASIATIC SOCIETY OF GREAT BRITAIN.—The scope of this small book is rightly expressed in its title. The author who is Lecturer in History in the Calcutta University, has collected and discussed statements, references, and allusions from the early literature to throw light on the position and life of Kṛṣṇa and the growth of Bhāgavatism. He deals with the various theories that have been put forward, and with good reasons discredits the views that Kṛṣṇa Vāsudeva was a solar deity or a tribal god or a vegetation deity. He is right in treating Kṛṣṇa Vāsudeva as one person, the Vṛṣṇi chief, but he unnecessarily identifies him with Kṛṣṇa Devakīputra, the scholar mentioned in the Chāndogya Upanishad........... (F. E. Pargiter).

THE BOMBAY CHRONICLE, JUNE 19, 1921.—In this small book of a hundred and seventeen pages, Mr. Hemchandra Ray Chaudhuri of the Calcutta University has collected much valuable material from which he has succeeded in tracing the origin and growth of the Vaishnava creed. The Historicity of Srikrishna—or as the author calls him, Krishna Vāsudeva, is also handled with remarkable clearness............

A. GOVINDACHARYA SVAMIN.—I pay you a most deserved compliment upon your acquaintance with the Azhvars and Sri Vaishnavism of Southern India as evidenced in your learned book *the Early History of the Vaishnava Sect.*

R. SHAMASASTRY, MYSORE.—You are a specialist in Vaishnavism.

III. Studies in Indian Antiquities

Demy 8vo. Pp. xvi, 211

Published by the Calcutta University

PROFESSOR E. J. RAPSON, CAMBRIDGE.—Dr. Raychaudhuri's essays on Indian History and Antiquities are always well-informed, thoughtful and suggestive.

E. J. THOMAS (J. R. A. S., OCTOBER, 1933, p. 925).—The study which Dr. Raychaudhuri has already devoted to ancient Indian history is well known. In the present book he discusses some of the geographical problems which still face the historians, as well as Vedic, epic, and specially historical questions......He has shown that Indian historical scholarship is proceeding on sound lines of its own and achieving independent results.

Opinions on some of the Papers incorporated in the Volume.

DR. BARNETT.—They are very interesting and critically sound.

DR. KEITH.—They are all very interesting, and I am glad to note the very useful information elicited as to Bhoja.

PROFESSOR DR. STEN KONOW, KRISTIANIA, NORWAY.—They are written in a thoroughly scholarlike way, and more especially it seems to me that your paper about the Laksmana Sena era deserves very careful attention.

PROFESSOR H. JACOBI.—The verification of the Bhāgavata credo in the Besnagar inscription is a find on which you may be congratulated.

PROFESSOR SCHRADER, KIEL, GERMANY.· *The Antiquity of the Rig Veda* is a sober and useful little piece of research work with which, on the whole, I fully agree. If we follow Jacobi and Tilak we create a gap (which we cannot bridge over) between the Mantras and the Brāhmanas, for the latter are certainly not far removed from early Buddhism. On the other hand, if Hertel were right, the Ṛg Veda would immediately precede Buddhism, and there would be no room at all for Brāhmanas and Upaniṣads.

Your important paper on the inter-relation of the two epics: The opinion held by Macdonell, Winternitz, and others, *viz.*, that the heroes of the Mahābhārata are unknown to the Rāmāyaṇa, seems, indeed, to be untenable... Again, I find it difficult, as you do, to distinguish between a Pāṇḍava story and a Kuru-Bhārata Epic.

PROFESSOR JARL CHARPENTIER.—The identification of some words in this very important document (the Besnagar Inscription) with a passage in the Mahābhārata seems to be a most happy find.

PROFESSOR E. WASHBURN HOPKINS.—It is certainly a remarkable resemblance which you have established and I should be inclined to agree with your conclusion

———